Girls' Night Out

Girls' Night Out

Having Fun with Your Daughter
While Raising a Woman of God

Michaelann Martin with MariAnna Martin

EMMAUS
ROAD
PUBLISHING

Steubenville, Ohio
A Division of Catholics United for the Faith
www.emmausroad.com

EMMAUS
ROAD
PUBLISHING

Emmaus Road Publishing
827 North Fourth Street
Steubenville, Ohio 43952

Cover and interior design by Julie Davis, General Glyphics, Inc., Dallas, Texas (www.glyphnet.com)

DEDICATION

To all mothers, especially my own.

Table of Contents

Acknowledgements ix

Introduction 1

1. Being an Awesome Daughter of God 11
    Tea party / St. Therese

2. Embrace Your Natural Beauty 21
    Facials / Blessed Mother Teresa

3. Supernatural Beauty Begins with a Relationship with
    God the Father 33
    A quiet place to pray / St. Rose of Lima

4. Beauty, Purity, and Modesty in Dress 43
    Bookstore and café / St. Maria Goretti

5. Mary as Our Mother and Model of Beauty 57
    Prayer walk / Blessed Virgin Mary

6. Fun and Faithful Fashion with Joy 65
    Shopping together / St. Gianna Beretta Molla

7. Virtuous Friendships 77
    Manicure and pedicure / St. Martha and St. Mary

8. Boys, Boys, Boys & Girls! 89
    Fitness center and smoothies / St. Francis and St. Clare

9. Embracing Womanhood and Exploring Vocational Options 103
    Dessert in a cozy café / St. Rita

10. Dress-up Date with Mom and Dad 115
    Fancy restaurant

Scriptural Rosary 125

On the Communion of Saints 129

ACKNOWLEDGMENTS

*I must express my deep gratitude
for all of the deposits of love my mother made
and continues to make in my life
and in the lives of my sisters and our daughters.*

*I would also like to thank MariAnna
for her willingness to have fun with me on our
dates and writing this book,
and to all of my sons for putting up with
the two silly girls in our family.*

*Most especially I am grateful to Curtis,
my wonderful husband, for raising our children
with me and always leading our family closer to
Christ. We could do nothing without
his love and support.*

Introduction

> *Let no one have contempt for your youth, but set an example for those who believe, in speech, conduct, love, faith and purity.*
> 1 Timothy 4:12

Why this guide? Because I am the mother of eight children. My husband and I have been blessed with seven sons and one daughter so far, so spending special time with my daughter, MariAnna, has been a particular joy for me. In a house filled with energy and masculine enthusiasm, we girls need to stick together in our home. Curtis and I have tried to make an effort to take each of our children out for "special time" each week, and taking *extra* special time in their preadolescent years to prepare them for adult life has proven to be a great adventure. My husband has been able to spend time with each of our sons preparing them for manhood, and I have been able to spend time with MariAnna.

We started by taking just one child with us on outings or errands and having spontaneous one-on-one conversations with them. These outings grew into planned conversations as each child grew in understanding and maturity. Now we have a set progression of ideas and talks planned in order to prepare them for adolescence and adult life. It is wonderful to have adult conversations with our teenaged children, and as a result they have begun thinking about morality and real life in very practical ways. I can't help but think that while this is due largely to God's grace, it is also partly a result of our willingness to *invest* in our relationships with our children.

Curtis and I have been gathering and reading parenting books since before the birth of our first son, so everything I will share with you was first shared with me.

This guide is a direct result of the special "girl time" that my mother made for my sisters and me. She gave me the gift of playing dress-up and having tea parties that I will never forget. I am grateful to my mother for taking the time to be not only a mom, but a special friend to me as a child, young woman, and now as a fellow mother. I have been able to spend time with my daughter MariAnna because my mother gave that gift to me many years ago.

MariAnna and I have had a lot of fun discussing our "girlness," as well as our special God-given gifts and roles. We have been at one another's side in writing this guide. There have been moments of giggles and silliness, and times of tears and embracing as we share ourselves in the text. I write *as* a mother *for* mothers, intending this guide to serve as an aid for discussing authentic femininity with your daughters. We are living in a day and age when we cannot assume that our values and faith are being taught to our daughters in school or in the world. As mothers, we have a tremendous responsibility to equip our daughters with the tools they will need to grow in femininity and in holiness.

Each of us has been created with the end in mind, destined for life in heaven with God for all eternity. With eyes fixed on this eternal goal, we must strive to raise our daughters to be women of God. It is my hope that this guide will encourage you to think about and discuss these topics which are *particular* to femininity. You may find that you have better ideas for "dates" than I've come up with, and that's great! You may discover more casual methods of integrating the "tough topics" into your regular conversations with your girls—that's even better.

The goal is for you to spend time with your daughter discussing the richness of our Catholic faith, and the particular charge that we, as women, have received to reflect His love to the world. There are sample discussions that are provided for you to review and modify for use within your own family, and I encourage you to make this material your own.

MariAnna and I have had the opportunity to live out all of these dates and ideas, and it is our hope that we can share the richness of the mother-daughter relationship with you. Since we discovered the joy of discussing these truly feminine topics together *before* she hit the raging rapids of puberty, when it did arrive, we had a foundational relationship sufficient to weather the storms. Our history of spending special time together ensured that when the worldly challenges arose, we were better equipped to work through them together—in love. Establishing a deeper relationship with MariAnna was a tremendous benefit of our mother-daughter dates; growing in our faith together was an even greater benefit.

You will notice that the last activity listed in this guide calls for a special dinner date with both mom *and* dad. Much research has been done lately on the importance of a father's role in his little girl's life. Our daughters need to know from the very beginning that they are daddy's little princesses, just as they are God the Father's little princesses. Your husband's participation in this "girl adventure" is critical. I have intentionally shared with Curtis details of the discussions and activities of these special mother-daughter dates so that he actually *is* involved. This way, when circumstances permit, he can present critical ideas and concepts from a "guy's" perspective for her.

These father-daughter conversations are invaluable to her growth as a woman. When a daughter not only *hears* of her father's love for her through his affirming words, but also tangibly *experiences* it through intimate conversation with him, she will be less likely to search for love and inappropriate intimacy with boys and young men from her peer group. When she feels that unconditional love from her dad, she also feels a sense of fulfillment, satisfying her need for love until full maturity allows for real discernment of her vocation.

We have had the great pleasure of talking with each child about all of life's issues, pinpointing changes on the horizon and sharing our experiences about grown-up life in general. As a family habit, we celebrate each child's passage from childhood into adulthood by going on a "Thirteen-Year-Old Trip." Years ago, someone told my husband that it would be a good idea to take each of our sons on a "rite of passage" trip to further cement their relationship. He took that advice to heart, and he has enjoyed some wonderful times with our sons so far. It was odd, because as a mother, I could see the great benefits of this male bonding time, but in my heart I too wanted to have that special time with each of my children. I knew I couldn't go on these trips with them, or it would wreck the important male dynamic.

> The goal is for you to spend time with your daughter discussing the richness of our Catholic faith, and the particular charge that we, as women, have received to reflect His love to the world.

My husband was very wise in sharing some great male insights with me. Thanking me for allowing him the opportunity to walk with our sons into manhood, he explained that the boys couldn't yet appreciate time with me, their mother, as they eventually would when they were more mature. They were still trying to figure out what being a young man of God was supposed to look like, and the process of separating themselves from their mother was going to be one of the greatest challenges of their adolescence.

Curtis shared one of his own adolescent memories with me, recalling a trip that he had taken with his own mother when he was eighteen. His grandfather was dying, and his father had asked him to accompany his mother to New Orleans to say one last goodbye to her father. He agreed to go despite the difficult relationship with his mother at that time, resigning himself to a torturous couple of weeks. But an amazing thing happened on that trip: removed from the burdens of daily life, he experienced an eye-opening, deeply enriching time with his mother. They were able to talk and laugh and enjoy each other's company, and he began to appreciate her and love her in a more meaningful way—in an adult way. Having lived this experience himself, he proposed that I take each of the boys on an "Eighteen-Year-Old Trip" when the time came, and said he would do the same with Marianna.

> The beauty and purpose of this guide is twofold, intending first to steep mothers in the awesomeness of their own femininity and in the wonder of being God's own daughter, and to then equip them with the tools to share these insights with their daughters.

I was thrilled at his suggestion, and still am. It gives me great joy to hear my older boys talk about what adventure they want to take their mom on when their eighteenth year comes around, and when MariAnna came to her thirteenth year, we decided to wait another year so that we can take extra time in planning the perfect trip for two.

More About Investing

Before we enter into our examination of the joys and benefits of spending constructive, quality time with our daughters, I would like to emphasize the concept of *investing* in our children. We live in an age where there are many demands on our children for their attention. If your children are in school, they spend most of the day in the care of other adults, some of whom do not share your attitudes, values, and morals. Having a large family has its own challenges as well. Trying to find one-on-one time with each child has been a struggle at times, but a struggle that we have chosen to regard as an adventure.

When our first child was born, we vowed to set aside quality time for him and each of our future children. We have often made sacrifices to build and maintain personal relationships with them. It is *crucial* that we invest in our children so that when the time comes for us to draw the line, whether morally or spiritually—and to perhaps go against the grain, countering the influence that others may have in our children's lives—we are able to speak to them with credibility and authority.

My husband explains it this way: We can think of our children as having "Relational Bank Accounts" within their very persons. It is our job as parents to make deposits into these accounts during their lifetimes. We have found a great resource in Gary Chapman, author of numerous books on the topic of "love languages." His books, *The Five Love Languages of Teenagers* and *The Five Love Languages of Children* are particularly useful tools in determining the primary "love language" or channel through which each child is predisposed to receive love. Depending on your daughter's dominant love language, you can tailor your expressions of love, showing and telling her in many ways that you love her. Each time you go out of your way to invest in your child, you are making a deposit. A lifetime of deposits makes for a very healthy "Relational Bank Account."

In adolescence, there will be times when mom and dad need to make withdrawals from the Relational Bank Account. For example, when we say, "You may not go to that party," or "You must be home by your curfew of 11:00," or "No, that concert is not a place for a lady," or make other unpopular decisions as parents must do, we are making withdrawals. These withdrawals may be difficult to make, and they can be a strain on healthy relationships, but that strain is precisely what builds strength and character.

When our Relational Bank Accounts with each of our children are well-funded, then the relationships can withstand the test of withdrawals. When we are not well-invested in our children, then those withdrawals can break relationships. We see this in many of the kids with whom we work on college campuses. They are badly wounded by parents who were trying to do the right thing for their children, but who ended up breaking the relationship because they failed to realize the importance of the Relational Bank Account, or else were dangerously overdrawn once the time came to switch roles from "friend" to "enforcer." That being said, these dates and times you spend with your daughter can yield rich deposits into your personal account with her.

The purpose of this guide is twofold: first, to immerse mothers in the beauty of their femininity and in the wonder of being daughters of God; second, to equip them with the tools to share these insights with their own daughters. We are living in an era when our girls do not hear often enough how wonderful they are or that by the very nature of their femininity they have a valuable role in God's plan for humanity.

This guide is divided into ten lessons that are accompanied by a date activity for you and your daughter to experience together. The purpose of the date is to spend time growing in your personal relationship, and to explore the wonders of being created female and being unique in God's eyes. They are fun and inexpensive ways to invest in your relationship with your daughter. Take these opportunities to talk through the changes and struggles that she might be experiencing now, or will be experiencing as she enters into womanhood.

Before you begin this journey together, it is a good idea to purchase two journals, which can be found at most bookstores. They will serve as tools to record personal thoughts or as prayer journals, preserving as treasured memories these wonderful times spent together as your daughter matures into the young woman that God has planned. You will want to purchase these before your first date together. You might want to write her name in calligraphy on the front, or decorate it with adjectives that describe and honor her as a young woman. A benefit to each of you having your own journal is that you will be growing *together* in your understanding of your femininity as mother and daughter, and journaling will allow you to grow closer to God in faith and prayer.

It is a wonderful gift from God to be a woman! I pray that this guide will be a tool to help you enjoy the talents and individuality of your daughter. When was the last time you thought of your femininity and your ability to carry and nurture life as a gift from God? It is a priceless gift, and we forget it all too often because this gift of love comes at a cost.

| A Few Words about Adolescence

Women experience fertility in different ways. Some have a cycle that brings a slight difference in mood or emotion, or a little physical discomfort; others suffer through days of severe pain and discomfort, possibly accompanied by a short temper or plain old irritability. While experiences differ, the reality of monthly changes is common. Just as we mothers experience ups and downs in our moods and emotions, we recognize that our daughters will also be boarding this emotional roller coaster at some point. Their little-girl bodies are going to come under chemical attack and their minds are going to be filled with new thoughts and impulses. Add to this experience the new volatility of emotions, and you have adolescence.

Our daughters may experience overwhelming emotions in the face of this transition, so the time to arm them with the truth to survive this tumultuous transition is now, before the onset of change! I began talking with my daughter about adolescence when she was eleven years old. By the time she was thirteen and her body was changing, she was ready for the challenges it brought, and able to look upon it as an adventure from God.

We can't fool ourselves into thinking that the tranquility of the early years is going to remain indefinitely—we need to prepare for the rapids of adolescence. Add to this the societal pressure that is placed on our young people and you could have tragedy if you don't take this seriously. I have heard a comparison made between life and a flowing river: the younger years are the slow, tranquil waters of a calm river, while the adolescent years are like the roaring rapids that begin at Class I and can get up to Class V around the next bend! Then, almost miraculously, the river flows smoothly again into adulthood. This image has given Curtis and me great strength, not only in planning and preparing for the rapids, but also in clinging to the knowledge that this rough time is not permanent, and that with a bit of a sporting spirit and a lot of prayer and parental love, we can make it through together. Adolescence is a critical time, but it doesn't have to leave you or your family in critical condition.

> The purpose of the date is to spend time growing in your personal relationship, and to explore the wonders of being created female and being unique in God's eyes.

So what might those large rocks responsible for creating your daughter's rapids look like? They may jut out in the form of hormonal and chemical changes within her developing body, or perhaps as an excessive food and/or body awareness (perhaps even leading to disordered exercise or eating). A disordered preoccupation with her body, an attraction to popular or trendy styles of clothing (which may be impure or unhealthy for her self-concept), and her feelings about boys and relationships can *all* cause rushing rapids.

Add to the mix an increased sensitivity to peer opinion and possible fears about not fitting into the mold of the world, along with the added irritability and discomfort that accompany menstruation each month, and you have an idea of how terrifying these rapids can be. Take courage! God has given us the knowledge to help our girls through this.

It is good to know that on average, most girls begin developing into young women between the ages of ten and thirteen. Some girls may even begin menstruating at age nine. This could be due to the presence of excessive amounts of female hormones given to livestock to induce milk production, or to chickens to produce larger breasts for more white meat. Whatever the cause, it is good to know that it is happening, and that it may cause or contribute to your daughter entering into puberty as early as fourth grade.

Along with menstruation, you might notice the following personality changes in your daughter: unpredictable emotional outbursts, inability to maintain focus on the task at hand, irritability, lack of self-confidence, mean-spiritedness, scattered or diminished interest in former hobbies or activities, and inconsistent eating habits. There is also a new awareness of her body and personal appearance. Our culture is so infatuated with the "perfect" body that scores of our young girls are falling prey to disorders such as bulimia (or binging and purging) and anorexia (excessive exercising and/or dieting or outright denial of food to the body). These disorders are actually more prevalent in the smartest and highest achievers during their early adolescent years. They affect about one percent of young women and are some of the most difficult psychiatric disorders to treat. (See www.anad.org for more information.)

> If they don't have the knowledge of being children of God and of the unique role they play in His plan, then they may find themselves lost and turn to the world in search of their place and direction.

Our girls are being fed a lie from hell about their beautiful bodies. We need to inform them of the true facts, pointing out that the average model today weighs 23 percent less than the average woman today.[1] By arming our daughters with the truth, we can work to counter a tragic trend illustrated by a recent Harvard study in which two-thirds of *underweight* twelve-year-old girls thought they were fat.[2]

As if the hormones and bodily changes were not enough, sudden infatuation with boys might follow. If your daughter doesn't seem to be interested yet, you can bet that it will hit when her circle of friends enters into the full swing of boy-craziness. This new awareness of boys creates an added confusion of how to act in mixed company, and can lead to an excessive preoccupation with boy/girl relationships and teen dating.

Serial dating, often leading to open sexual activity among teens, should be of grave concern to parents. In fact, the whole idea of dating seems inappropriate when you look at the number of young girls, ages twelve to thirteen, with multiple sexual partners and having babies of their own. The likelihood of teen sexual activity increases when kids spend six months or more in an "exclusive relationship."[3] We can't think of this as harmless "puppy love" anymore. Along with this obsession with romantic boy-girl relationships, our girls are encouraged through popular television shows, music, and teen magazines to do the asking and paying, inadvertently robbing their future husbands of the opportunities to be brave and to have to pursue or *court* the woman of their dreams. It is up to us as moms to escort our daughters into this new world with grace.

Our young people don't know where they fit in or where they belong in society. If they don't have the knowledge of being children of God and of the unique role they play in His plan, then they may find themselves lost and turn to the world in search of their place and direction.

But what do they find? Celebrities who are popular, wealthy, and professing great happiness, but who are in reality addicted to drugs, lost in total self-gratification, and withering away into despair and gloom. Our young people may choose to imitate them anyway. They dress like celebrities, they utter the phrases they hear spoken on MTV, and they consume that which the world promises as fulfilling—totally disregarding their dignity as human persons—only to find that these promises are empty.

We need to introduce our daughters to the beauty and dignity they possess as God's daughters. It is our job to arm them with the truth contained in His Word: the *Holy Bible*. Throughout this guide, you and I are going to focus on your daughter's body image, her perception of her own worth, and how she will choose to present and live out God's truth in her young-adult life. This will not only equip her to live as an awesome daughter to her earthly parents, but it will encourage her to strengthen her relationship with her Heavenly Father as well.

It might be a challenge to carve out time for your daughter. It's not enough just to have her accompany you on the usual errands and carpooling—you must take time to actually prepare your thoughts for these dates and discussions and make yourself attentive and exclusively available to your daughter. Looking at her and listening to her when she speaks, or engaging in *active* listening, is a wonderful posture to strive for. Talking about critical issues will bond you to one another, strengthening your relationship for all eternity. This connection with your daughter will be of great value to her as she navigates the rapids of adolescence.

I have included references to the best books and resources that I have found on the topics covered in each chapter. I hope you are able to take some time to go deeper and read the ones that apply to your own needs and concerns. I encourage you to look over the discussion topics and corresponding suggested activities. (It will only take a short time to read through the text before you make plans to go out together.) Your daughter may not recognize or acknowledge this portion of your investment in her, but your time and conversation together will be more fruitful when you do. You need only be one chapter ahead of each activity so that the discussion topic is fresh in your mind. Think of this as a wonderful opportunity to take our Blessed Mother's hand, joining with her to usher your daughter into womanhood.

> It is up to us as moms to escort our daughters into this new world with grace.

Lesson 1
Being an Awesome Daughter of God

You are His Princess

When I was a young girl, the Prince of Wales, Prince Charles, was looking for a suitable wife to be his princess, and all of the media was watching him. It so happened that he found a beautiful young maiden named Diana who was not a full princess, but who had enough royal blood in her to make her a suitable partner for the prince. She was very pretty, and it was no surprise that they began to spend some time together and eventually fell in love with one another.

A strange thing began to happen as their relationship grew. The Queen Mother, Prince Charles's mum, stepped in to give young Diana some official training in royalty. You see, though Diana possessed some royal blood, she had lived her early life as a commoner and needed to spruce up her manners and her conduct in order to behave in a way befitting a princess. The media had a field day with this; they photographed Diana being taught how to walk like a true lady, how to dress with dignity and honor, how to talk and have conversations fitting for a princess, and even how to wave to the crowds of onlookers.

I am sure that Diana found this quite exhausting, but she wanted to learn so that she could become the best possible princess. *The Princess Diaries* is a bit of a spoof on a similar situation: Young Mia, living the life of an American teenager, is notified by her heretofore unknown grandmother that she is, in fact, a European princess. Mia reluctantly moves to her native country for training in the art of living like a princess. Again, the Queen Mother takes the

> Like fine china, women are
> unique, priceless, and precious.

young princess under her wing and gently teaches her the manners and life of a royal. Both of these young women-turned-princesses come to find out that to live as royalty is both a great honor *and* a great responsibility.

In a similar way, we as Christians are invited into a royal family. The royal kingdom of God is the family into which we are each made members at our Baptism:

> The baptized have become "living stones" to be "built into a spiritual house, to be a holy priesthood." [1 Pet 2:5] By Baptism they share in the priesthood of Christ, in his prophetic and royal mission. They are "a chosen race, a royal priesthood, a holy nation, God's own people, that [they] may declare the wonderful deeds of him who called [them] out of darkness into his marvelous light" [1 Pet 2:9] (CCC 1268).

The indelible mark of priest, prophet, and king is made upon our heart and soul at the moment of our baptism, and it is our life-long mission to live out these three roles as members of God's family.

Think first for a moment about the role of the priest: his mission is to bring God to people. This is true of the priests in the Old Testament—where some priests literally had face-to-face conversations with God—and it is true of priests today, who bring Jesus to us in a miraculous way through the consecration of the Holy Eucharist in the celebration of the Mass.

The second identifying baptismal mark is that of prophet, or one who witnesses by his words. A prophet tells others about God. The prophets of the Old Testament gave hope to the Israelite people as they struggled to find God, and modern day prophets do the same for people who have lost contact with or sight of God in our world. Prophets bring God's good news in His words, spoken through them, and in the reality of the way they live their lives in imitation of Him.

Lastly, we have the mark of king. So what about kings? Most of us do not live under a monarchy, so the concept of royalty might seem a bit foreign, but there are many great and holy kings and queens in the Scriptures and modern history. We just need to turn back the clock in search of holy royalty. Kings, queens, princes, and princesses have a great responsibility to rule with dignity, honor, and justice, as well as to serve as Christ, our king, modeled. That is a tall order for anyone, and to do it well is a great accomplishment. Our "kingliness," or royal mark, is one indicative of great dignity as well. We are told in the New Testament about the immeasurable honor inherent in our own royal call:

> *See what love the Father has given us, that we should be called children of God; and so we are.* 1 John 3:1 RSV*

> *For those who are led by the Spirit of God are children of God. For you did not receive a spirit of slavery to fall back into fear, but you received a spirit of adoption, through which we cry, "Abba Father!" The Spirit itself bears witness with our spirit that we are children of God and if children, then heirs, heirs of God and joint heirs with Christ, if only we suffer with him so that we may also be glorified with him.* Romans 8:14–17

We are made daughters of God through our baptism. We now have a royal responsibility to His royal family—we have become ambassadors for God's kingdom here on earth! We now have a duty: to live not as commoners of the world, but as the princesses that we truly are, to live lives of justice and charity, always striving to bring more people into God's family—these must be our new goals. We may want to consider whether we, like Princess Diana or Princess Mia, might need some Royalty 101 training ourselves.

God in His wisdom knew that we would need help in relearning our royal roots, so He gave us the greatest Queen Mother possible: the Blessed Virgin Mary. Our Mother Mary is our mentor for living feminine holiness in our royal roles as daughters of God. Let's remember that she lived in such union with God in both study and prayer that she was able to say "yes" to His proposal that she become the mother of Jesus. Her life was a witness to her faith and trust in God (her role as a prophet for God), and she was the one who brought Jesus, the Son of God and King of Kings, into this world (her royal priestly mission). There is no better mentor for women to learn from.

Mary *wants* to guide us as we discover our own personal roles in this mission and as we help our daughters discover their roles as well. She wants to bring Jesus to us so that we can give Him to others. What gifts we have been given in our faith and in the Catholic Church! We are embarking upon a wonderful time not only of *self*-discovery but of *mutual* discovery with our daughters. Together we are Awesome Daughters of God!

---

* Revised Standard Version

Girls' Night Out #1
Plan a special Tea Party with your daughter!

God knew us before we were conceived!

> *Before I formed you in the womb I knew you.* Jeremiah 1:5

> *Yet, O LORD, you are our father; we are the clay and you the potter: we are all the work of your hands.* Isaiah 64:8

When I was a child, I had many physical deformities on my legs and hands. I found myself the butt of many unkind jokes and the object of ridicule. When I would come home from school in tears after being made fun of, my mother would hold me and tell me that I was a beautiful gift from God, that He made me for a very special purpose, and that my suffering some ridicule was part of His larger plan. She told me that He was there to help me through the difficult times, and that all I had to do was ask Him for help and for the grace to weather the storms of life. I took her advice, and each episode seemed to hurt a little less. I didn't fully understand His plan, but I began to trust in His fatherly love for me.

Not too long ago, a friend emailed me this analogy and it seems to fit perfectly with the message you will give to your daughter on your first date together.

There is a great difference in drinking out of a Starbucks paper cup and a fine bone china cup, isn't there? The one is very common and disposable. It comes in 200-cup tubes, has an extra heat sleeve, is most likely made out of 60% recyclable material, and is normally thrown in the trash. The other is so fine and valuable that it is usually placed on a special shelf or in a china hutch to protect it from being broken. It is irreplaceable and warrants special care. Many tea cups are hand blown and individually hand painted. Of these there are no two alike, for they are each unique.

We want to use this analogy to express the uniqueness and ultimate value that your daughter has in God's creation. She is not like the Starbucks cup that has little value and can be tossed away. She is *unique* and *priceless*. Her value is intrinsic to her personhood. God made her exactly the way she is for a reason, and it will be a great adventure to embark on a journey toward growing in grace.

WHERE TO GO

Make reservations to have High Tea at a local tea house or a special restaurant. (You can look in the phone directory for potential sites such as a bed and breakfast or various fine hotels if you don't have a tearoom in your area.) The idea is that you want to go to a place where you will be served lavish appetizers or desserts with tea in fine china cups and saucers. It is important to have quality in the service in order to drive home the idea that your daughter is priceless and unique. She is a royal Daughter of God, and therefore treating her with reverence and honor is a must. When you call ahead for reservations, you will want to ask about the fine china. If the establishment doesn't have bone china, ask permission to bring your own so that your point can be well made. Let your daughter know about the date, and encourage her to dress up to go out with you. Plan a special outfit for yourself to let her know that this is a grand occasion that you are looking forward to.

WHAT TO BRING

You will want to bring china cups and saucers if needed, and a paper cup and a plain ceramic mug for the sake of conversation. Also bring the two new journals with new pens and be prepared to present your daughter with hers as a gift. You might want to purchase a holy card of St. Therese to keep as a bookmark and prayer reminder in her journal.

Make an effort to purchase some rose oil of St. Therese or special rose-scented lotion or perfume before you go on your date.

GIRL TALK

Once you are seated, take out your St. Therese rose oil or rose-scented lotion or perfume and spritz some on your daughter's wrists. Let her know that her value and beauty are beyond measure and that the luxury of the rose oil is well-deserved. She is like a beautiful rose bud in God's garden and it will be a great joy to watch her grow into full bloom. Once your tea arrives, your time of fellowship and treats will begin. Now is the time for you to share some thoughts with your daughter. Share the Scripture verses in the text and let her know that this is a special time for both of you—getting dressed up is always fun and festive. Ask her how she feels or what she is thinking of your date so far. Hopefully she will be feeling special and excited to be out with you.

Finally, take out your mug and paper cup and put them on the table. Ask her if she would have felt as special if you had gone to a Denny's or a fast food joint for a quick cup of hot cocoa. Be sure to stress how special she is to you, as well as her priceless worth beyond measure! Let her know that she has great value in God's eyes.

God is the potter and we are the clay, but not just any common clay. We are like the fine china cups that we are drinking from. God has created us each unique, and He continues to mold us into the daughters and women that He wants us to be. Each one of us is a masterpiece of God's, no matter how often we forget about being special and we revert to acting like a paper cup or a common mug. Ask your daughter if she can give some examples of situations where we as women act "common." She might say that some people act common or cheap in the way that they dress or speak, or even by the way they act. All of these are true, and it will be helpful for the two of you to discuss how each of you might live more like the precious piece of china instead of as a mug or a paper cup.

JOURNAL TIME

At this point you can present your daughter with the gift of her journal and pen. You might want to say the prayer to St. Therese on the back of her prayer card and ask her to be your guide as you grow in grace together.

The following list is for you to copy into your journals and go through individually and then together. In each situation, the idea is to ask whether you resemble a paper cup (peasant behavior), a ceramic mug (the behavior of a commoner), or a fine china cup (the royal Daughter of God who you truly are).

Copy the list below into your journal writing "P" (Paper cup or Peasant), "C" (Ceramic mug or Commoner), and "FC/RD" (Fine China or Royal Daughter of God) after each statement to represent how you live each statement at this time in your life. After completing the list, talk about your findings with each other.

After taking this quiz together, discuss ways that you might move toward living as a Royal Daughter of God in the areas that you scored as "peasant" or "commoner." This way, when taking

Behavior Statement:
(Add the letter that describes your current behavior.)

- ❧ How I care for my hygiene, hair, & skin
- ❧ How I care for my body
- ❧ How I act with my family members
- ❧ How I act with my friends
- ❧ How I act with those I don't like
- ❧ How I speak to members of my family
- ❧ How I speak to adults
- ❧ How I speak to and with my friends
- ❧ How I pray and speak to God
- ❧ How I attend Mass
- ❧ How I dress for school
- ❧ How I want to dress
- ❧ What I watch on T.V.
- ❧ What movies I watch in the theater
- ❧ What movies I want to see
- ❧ What books I read
- ❧ What magazines and catalogues I look at
- ❧ The people that I am attracted to are…
- ❧ My friends tend to lead me toward…

notes during prayer time it is easy to be reminded of the areas where one is striving for improvement.

Share the following scripture verses with your daughter and have her copy them into her journal. The hope is that she will return to them later in prayer and reflect on being an Awesome Daughter of God.

> *See what love the Father has given us, that we should be called children of God; and so we are.* 1 John 3:1 RSV

> *For those who are led by the Spirit of God are children of God. For you did not receive a spirit of slavery to fall back into fear, but you received a spirit of adoption, through which we cry, "Abba Father!" The Spirit itself bears witness with our spirit that we are children of God and if children, then heirs, heirs of God and joint heirs with Christ, if only we suffer with him so that we may also be glorified with him.* Romans 8:14–17

Be sure to tell your daughter how proud of her you are and how special your time together is. Let her know what a great gift God's Fatherly love for her truly is, and encourage her never to be afraid to approach her loving Father. Remind her that we *all* struggle to live as awesome daughters of God, but that "with God all things are possible."[4]

After such intimate conversation, you will be able to encourage each other and hold each other accountable when you see one another falling short of your resolutions. This is a wonderful time to adopt a sporting spirit about growing in holiness together in the world.

PRAYER TIME

Conclude your date by taking a few minutes after you reach home to hold hands and pray together. It is a great idea to begin your vocal prayer by greeting God the Father and honoring Him. Thank Him for the gift of your daughter and the gift of your femininity. Thank Him for the time you have shared with your daughter on this date and ask Him to bless her as she grows in grace and womanhood. Thank Him for the gift of Jesus and ask Jesus to walk with you and your daughter daily.

Invite your daughter to pray as well, and close your prayer by asking the Holy Spirit to send His gifts upon you as you embark upon this journey. End your time together by reading a short essay on the life of St. Therese, asking her to help you see your femininity as God does, and asking our Blessed Mother to walk with you and your daughter. In closing, you can recite the prayer to St. Therese on the back of your holy card.

IDEAS FOR BONDING AFTER YOUR DATE

- ⚜ Purchase a silver tea set as an heirloom and reminder to your daughter of her femininity and unique beauty in God's eyes.
- ⚜ Purchase a delicate china cup and saucer set to display in a prominent place in your home or daughter's room.
- ⚜ Read about our Super Model: St. Therese of the Child Jesus.
- ⚜ Watch the St. Therese movie together and talk about her life.
- ⚜ Read together *The Story of a Soul*, by St. Therese of Lisieux.
- ⚜ Read *God Thinks You're Wonderful*, by Max Lucado.

SUPER MODEL
St. Therese of the Child Jesus

Many of you know that St. Therese was a young woman who gave her life to Christ by joining the Carmelite order when she was fifteen. She was the youngest of five girls, though her saintly parents lost four children at early ages, making a total of nine Martin children.

Therese lost her mother when she was just four years old, and suffered another emotional blow when her closest sister entered the cloister when she was eight. Therese, also known as The Little Flower of Jesus, had to learn how to die to herself and live for God—and His will—at an early age. In the many books about Therese, we learn that she was an astonishingly beautiful little girl. People would stop on the street and stare at her long blonde hair that was curled every morning. Her father fancied it that way and taught her to love beauty. Thanks to this sensitivity, she was able to see beauty in nature and in people. Therese had a tremendous appreciation for beauty in art and in the created world, always directing the glory to God the Father. She was a princess of God.

Her older sisters taught her about the child Jesus. She used to think of Jesus having her as His little ball or toy whom He could toss about or just set in the corner and ignore, and she would be happy just being His. She later began to meditate on the Holy Face of Jesus and she grieved over the great agonies that He endured for love of each one of us. Jesus gave her insight into having zeal to save souls—all souls. She would offer even the smallest of sacrifices for the sake of the poor souls who didn't know Christ, or for those in purgatory.

Therese had ambitions of traveling to foreign countries on missions to evangelize those without faith, but God had other plans for her. Her health began to fail when she was in her early twenties, and she remembers giving her will to God the Father and asking Him to fill her with His own will. She was able to have great joy in the midst of suffering and pain. She is quoted as saying that she desired to spend eternity "doing good in heaven for those on earth." She is one of three female doctors of the Church and is the patroness of Missionaries.

Lesson 2
Embrace Your Natural Beauty

The main goal of this chapter and date is to give our daughters a sense of who they are as daughters of God. God, our Father, has made each one of us unique and beautiful in His image and likeness. We need to celebrate this with our daughters, and learning about St. Therese is a great way to begin the celebration!

In *The Story of a Soul*, St. Therese gives us a beautiful image that Christ gave to her in explanation of God's indiscriminate gifts of grace to some with more abundance and with less to others. She recalls,

> *He opened the book of nature before me, and I saw that every flower He has created has a beauty of its own; that the splendor of the rose and the lily's whiteness do not deprive the violet of its scent, nor make less ravishing the daisy's charm. I saw that if every little flower wished to be a rose, nature would lose her spring adornments, and the fields would no longer be enameled with their varied flowers.*

So it is in the world of souls, the living garden of the Lord. It pleases Him to create great saints, who may be compared with the lilies or the rose; but He has also created little ones, who must be content to be daisies or violets nestling at His feet to delight His eyes when He should choose to look at them. The happier they are to be as He wills, the more perfect they are.

Have you ever been in a garden in spring? It is glorious to see and smell all of the beautiful flowers as they bloom. Some have fully bloomed while others are still young blossoms. And there are also those yet to blossom, still tiny buds. All are exquisite! This is true with our girls as well. They have a God-given gift of beauty and femininity, as do each of their mothers. We are each beautiful by our very nature—God made us this way. And yet, we are reminded countless times in Scripture not to get caught up in our physical beauty, but to develop our inner beauty for love of God. This is very true, but before we dig deeper into that truth we want to meet our daughters where they live: in the world. We want to celebrate their natural beauty traits and build up their God-given dignity and self confidence within each one.

Our true beauty—that which is everlasting—is found in our character, the love within our hearts, and the beauty of our souls. It is evident in the way we live each day, striving to seek union with God and accommodation to His will rather than catering to the will of the world. As mature adults, we may find it easier to grasp this thought than our daughters will, but we will take time in this chapter and date to better explain this wonderful vision to them, building up their self-image and their understanding of their own beauty.

> *Sixty queens there may be, and eighty concubines, and virgins beyond number; but my dove, my perfect one, is unique.*
> Song of Songs 6:8–9, NIV*

Do you realize that you are from God a gift beyond value? That you are unique and beautiful in your very being? This is true of *each* of us. Our daughters are living in a culture that is forcing physical beauty and a false body image upon them constantly; we need to fortify them with the armor of God. We want them to know that girls and women come in many shapes, sizes, and colors, and that God loves each one for her individuality and inner beauty. Just as St. Therese described the many flowers in the garden, we are each unique and beautiful in God's eyes. This date will allow you to focus on the *interior* beauty as well as the *external* physical beauty of your daughter.

Please reflect on the following before you begin this date with your daughter: we are in the midst of a war. Satan wants our daughters to find their self-worth in the things of the world, but God's plan for giving self-worth is very different.

The world would like us to look for self-worth in three main areas, and many of us fall prey to these each day. We are told that we derive our self-

---

* New International Version

worth from what we look like, by what we do (our careers), and by what others think about us.

First let's examine the idea of finding our self-worth in our appearance. The media and fashion industry bombard us with unreasonable images daily, creating the expectation that we look like these excessively skinny models and actresses. The effects of these abnormal images being thrust upon us and our daughters are measurable; studies have shown that women who look at advertisements filled with thin and beautiful women showed more signs of depression and were more dissatisfied with their own bodies after only *one to three minutes* of viewing the pictures.[5] Think how many images you and your daughter take in on a daily basis!

This same depressive effect can be noted in the consumption of fashion magazines and television. Some experiments show that viewing super-thin models increases the incidence of stress, depression, guilt, shame, and general body-dissatisfaction. (We will take some time on this date to look at current magazines with our daughters and directly refute the cultural lies that are presented in glossy print.)

The next area of unreality forced upon us by the media and worldly influences is the idea that *what we do* determines the value of *who we are*. Many adults—young and old alike—have bought into this criterion for self-worth; just think about the demands for social acceptance based upon accomplishment. Some might find self-worth in getting good grades or in being a popular cheerleader. Others might find their worth in the boardroom or on the trading floor. As parents, we too fall prey to this when we revert to the practice of listing off our accomplishments when meeting new people, as if presenting our resume will help them to accept and like us. This feeds into a dysfunctional means of determining self-worth based upon what others think about us.

Vanity and pride are two strong vices that can creep into our lives if we are not careful to keep them in check. Vanity, or thinking too much about one's self and what others might be thinking of you, is highly compatible with pride, or thinking one is greater than others or not caring enough about other's needs. These are forms of self-absorption and self-love. When we are vain we become like puppets, acting in ways designed to elicit the approval of other human beings instead of the approval of God. We are fearful of the possible disapproval of our peers or of the corrupt culture.

When we are filled with pride, we tend to act solely in accordance with our own ideas and desires, disregarding God's will in preference for our own. Take a moment and think about these pressures in your own life, discerning how you find your self-worth. (We will cover these topics in greater detail in Lesson 7: Virtuous Friendships. Be willing to share your own struggles with your daughter when you talk about these issues.)

There is good news: God's formula for finding our self-worth is a complete gift He offers us each day. We find our self-worth in *who* we are as His daughters, chosen and made for greatness. And the best part is that God is concerned primarily with our hearts. He loves us unconditionally, even when we have that large, unsightly pimple on our nose. He loves our heart, our soul, our inner being, and that is His gift to each of us. He gives us His grace and fatherhood, equipping us with the total confidence and self-worth that is needed to live with joy in this world. It is our duty to teach this to our girls.

Some words of wisdom:

> *The ways of the Lord are not comfortable, but we are not created for comfort, but for greatness and goodness.* Pope Benedict XVI
>
> *While we were still sinners Christ died for us.* Romans 5:8
>
> *For God so loved the world that he gave his only Son, so that everyone who believes in him might not perish but might have eternal life.* John 3:16

Girls' Night Out #2
Facials for Two

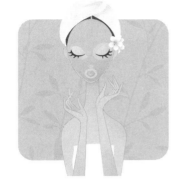

WHERE TO GO

Somewhere special for a facial (i.e., a candlelit bathroom or professional salon).

WHAT TO BRING

- Purchase a popular teen magazine or check one out at the library to view and discuss on you date.
- This book, *Girls' Night Out*.
- A bouquet of mixed flowers for your daughter.
- Journals

This date will take you and your daughter to a salon, department store, or a very clean bathroom (made special with candles, pretty scents, and products for facials). If you decide to break the bank and go to a salon for a professional facial, take a little time to talk before you get there. If you are on a tighter budget there are other options: many department stores have make-up counters like Clinique that have a "facial quota" to fill, so they do a certain number of facials each day. Another option might be a beauty college or academy in your town.

Making arrangements to get a skin care class and makeover is another option if you are looking to get out yet not spend too much money. My personal favorite is doing facials at home. My daughter and I purchased a home facial kit at our local health store (or try a pharmacy) and we had a wonderful retreat together without even leaving home!

I made sure our main bathroom was sparkling clean and lit candles. We brought in a comfy chair and bar stool and locked the door for our hour-long "getaway." If you are not comfortable doing this on your own, you could always schedule a visit from a Mary Kay (www.marykay.com) or Arbonne consultant (www.arbonne.com) to come give the two of you a skin care class. Both have skin care lines made especially for teens. However you decide to partake in this date, enjoy the time with your daughter. Celebrate being women of God together! Celebrate your natural beauty and unique traits while teaching the proper care for the body God has given each one of us. Remember the analogy of being exquisite "fine china" and not a common "paper cup." Our physical body is God's temple, the dwelling place of His Holy Spirit, chosen and purchased at a great price. We need to care for our skin, hair, and body so that we can be the best possible ambassadors for the Faith.

If you are doing this at home, try to take a little extra time to prepare a special iced tea or fruit juice spritzer (made with 1 part juice, any flavor, and 1 part 7Up) before you retreat into your spa oasis. If you are going out for facials, you might want to stop by a juice bar for refreshments while you peruse your magazines and discuss these topics with your daughter. While preparing for your facial, or even during your masks, you can begin to look at a popular teen magazine and discuss the crazy clothes and extremely thin bodies of the models. Be open and honest with your daughter about your own struggles to want to look good and fit in, or to be found thin and attractive. Discuss God's unconditional love for each one of us as we are.

Finally, present her with the bouquet of flowers and read her the quote from St. Therese about each flower being unique and special—created for a purpose all its own.

GIRL TALK

Make sure you share the basics of proper skin care and try to commit to the following:

- ⚜ Wash your face at least once a day with warm water and a wash cloth.
- ⚜ Be very gentle with the skin around the eyes.
- ⚜ Avoid touching your face with your hands.
- ⚜ Always brush your teeth in the morning and at night before bed.

Be sure to emphasize that wearing make-up is not necessary to enhance her natural beauty at this age. The time will come when she will be able to wear mascara, lip gloss, or whatever you decide is appropriate. We don't want our daughters growing up too soon or wishing away the beautiful innocence of their girlhood. Let your daughter know that she is beautiful exactly the way she is. Explain to her that God will send the right guy in *His* time, if she is called to marriage: one who will be attracted to her inner beauty *and* her outer beauty—all in His time. (We will cover the topic of boys in greater detail in future chapters.)

Talk about current trends in fashion, good and bad. Strategize how to be stylish and not show too much skin or over-emphasize certain body parts just because it's "trendy."

ONE POSSIBLE CONVERSATION MIGHT GO LIKE THIS:

Mom: "When you look through magazines or watch TV shows, do you find yourself thinking, "Wow, I wish I looked like her," then thinking about all of the things about yourself that aren't quite good enough or pretty enough? Be honest."

Daughter: "Yeah, sometimes."

Mom: "Me too."

Daughter: "Really?"

Mom: "Absolutely. This is because we are female! Our hearts seek beauty, love, and approval. We were made for relationship. You know there is NOT another girl out there in the whole world that is exactly like you. You are fantastic and unique!"

This might also be a good time to talk about anorexia and bulimia and their tragic results. I was hesitant to bring this up with my daughter, and I was shocked to hear that she, with her eighty-pound frame, shares the all too common feminine fear of being "fat."

In *Mom's Everything Book for Daughters*, Becky Freeman suggests this simple explanation:

> *Being a preteen girl can be tough, and sometimes girls who are healthy try to lose weight even though they don't need to. You may feel a lot of pressure to look a certain way. Acting on this pressure may lead to eating disorders like anorexia and bulimia nervosa.*

Anorexia nervosa is a form of self-starvation where a person does not eat enough food to keep healthy and does not maintain a healthy weight. Bulimia nervosa is when a person eats a lot of food and then vomits or uses other methods, such as fasting or exercising too much, to avoid gaining weight after overeating.

If you ever start thinking that you want to look and feel better, talk to me, and we can work together as a team to make small changes in our family eating and physical activity habits-without going overboard. Okay?

Make sure that you regularly compliment your daughter on specific unique traits she has. It might be her beautiful hair or perfect eyes. Ask her if there is something she is especially sensitive about and then console her in that area. Prepare her for the body changes that are to come such as wider hips, developing breasts, and the presence of body hair. Let her know that this is all a normal part of God's plan and not to be afraid. If her body is already changing, then celebrate it all the more. Try to say something positive to your daughter every day!

JOURNAL TIME

Take some time to tell your daughter about her unique beauty. Mom should have some positive things to say about her daughter. Here are just a few aspects to consider in your quest for crafting the perfect compliment for your princess: her hair, her eyes, her nose, her teeth, her face, her complexion, her skin, her smile, her physique, her height, her chest, her legs, her hands, her heart; then add a statement about what physical trait makes her most unique.

After hearing mom's compliments, it will be easier for her to write some personal statements on her own. In *Anne of Green Gables*, Anne was able to express that she really loved her nose, but *hated* her red hair. Your daughter needs to know that it is okay to feel these feelings. Remember that after Anne dyed her hair green, red didn't seem so bad! Our likes and dislikes are relative. Have her write your words in her journal, and also record some areas she likes and dislikes about herself. She can always go back and read what it was at this particular time in her life that she liked or disliked.

Do your best to encourage your daughter to let go of excessive vanity or concern about what others think of her. Teach her to accept her body as God created it and make a vow together to become the best versions of yourselves!

PRAYER TIME

Take a few minutes after wrapping up your facials to pray together. Express your thanksgiving to God the Father for the unique gift of your daughter, and pray for the grace to live as He has created his awesome royal daughters to do. Pray for special grace for your daughter to be confident in herself, especially in the area where she feels most insecure. Close by reading the short essay on the life of Blessed Mother Teresa.

IDEAS FOR BONDING AFTER YOUR DATE

- Read Super Model: Blessed Mother Teresa.
- Shop at a craft store for glitter signs to put on her bedroom door to remind your daughter just how great she is to you and to God! We found, "fabulous, beautiful, wonderful."
- Take a walk together.
- Schedule a weekly date to play tennis together.
- Go rollerblading together.
- Plan a garden and work in it together.
- Read or watch *Little Women* and/or *Anne of Green Gables* together.

SUPER MODEL
Blessed Mother Teresa

Mother Teresa was born Agnes Gonxha Bojaxhiu in Skopje, Macedonia (formerly Yugoslavia). Her parents, Nikola and Dranafile, were originally from Albania. Her father was a successful merchant and her mother stayed at home to care for her children: Lazar, a son, and two daughters, Agatha and *Gonxha* (which means "rosebud"). She grew up in a loving home where music and hospitality were abundant. We are told that her parents would often have poor strangers at family meals; their generosity helped form Mother Teresa's heart. The family lived quite comfortably, but as is the case with so many saints, sadness came into Gonxha's life early; her father died unexpectedly when she was only eight.

After Nikola died, Gonxha continued to be an excellent student and became very active in her parish. The parish priest, Father Franjo Jambrekovich, SJ, introduced the boys and girls to many new activities to help them grow in holiness and Gonxha embraced them. Fr. Franjo would often inspire his young followers by quoting St. Ignatius of Loyola, "What have I done for Christ? What am I doing for Christ? What will I do for Christ?" Because she spoke Serbo-Croatian, Albanian, and Latin, Gonxha was asked by Father Franjo to become his translator. She agreed and learned the catechism quite well by doing this. Her love for God and her ardent desire to serve others grew as she read about St. Ignatius's missions in India. She had a great respect for the Jesuit priests and for St. Ignatius especially.

Gonxha felt God calling her to serve Him through teaching, in a similarly radical way as had the missionaries whose stories she was reading. After much prayer and discernment, Gonxha asked her priest to help her apply to become a missionary herself. She found the Sisters of the Institute of the Blessed Virgin Mary (also called the Sisters of Loreto), an order that based their vocation and charism on the writings of St. Ignatius of Loyola. They were teachers engaged in mission work in India, and Gonxha knew that this was the order for her. She was sent to Ireland as a postulant and learned English while in her period of discernment there. When she moved to Darjeeling, India, she became a novice and Gonxha took the name Teresa after the French saint,

Therese of the Child Jesus (Therese of Lisieux). Another sister also wanted the name "Therese," so Gonxha elected to spell her religious name "Teresa," using the Spanish spelling.

Sister Teresa loved her work teaching in Calcutta and was soon elevated to mother superior of the high school and made the head of the Daughters of Loreto, native sisters she taught in Bengali. Now "Mother" Teresa, she continued in obedience to her rule but began to feel a strong desire to help the poor by doing more than teaching. In 1946, after much prayer, discernment, and counsel, Mother Teresa felt "a call within a call," to live among the poorest of the poor in Calcutta, offering free services to the most needy. She formed the Missionaries of Charity, but didn't receive official permission to be uncloistered (or active) and to begin her work until August of 1948.

Mother Teresa is known for her constant service to the poor and those in need. She relied on God to provide for her needs and the needs of those whom she served. The Missionaries of Charity are responsible for taking care of the homeless, orphans, lepers, and the dying. Her mission was to love as Christ loves and to see Christ in every soul in need of help. Smart and confident in being the woman God created her to be, she is a true supermodel for all women to imitate.

Lesson 3
Supernatural Beauty Begins with a Relationship with God the Father

Let not yours be the outward adorning with braiding of hair, decoration of gold, and wearing of clothing, but let it be the hidden person of the heart with the imperishable jewel of a gentle and quiet spirit, which in God's sight is very precious.
1 Peter 3:3–4, RSV

Where does real beauty come from? As women, we sometimes focus only on external beauty, the beauty that comes from sporting the most fashionable clothing, or the newest hairstyle, or fancy shoes. We are challenged to find the balance between embracing our God-given beauty and femininity without neglecting our supernatural beauty that lies in our inner character and life of virtue. In order to maintain this balance, we have to realize that true beauty comes from within; your outward appearance will reflect your inner beauty. Do we spend more time in front of the mirror making ourselves look externally beautiful than we do in front of God developing our inner beauty?

We know that we were made *for* God *by* God to be *with* God for all eternity, right? Well, in order to get to know Him more intimately, we need to spend time with Him. The challenge will be to spend more time and effort working on our internal beauty than on our external beauty. Just as young lovers want to spend every waking moment together, so too God wants to be with each one of us, constantly. He loves us more than we can imagine, but He is not going to push Himself on us; rather, He waits for us to come to Him.

Jesus tells us about the need we have to live in union with God the Father, God the Son, and God the Holy Spirit in this way:

> *"I am the true vine, and my Father is the vine grower. He takes away every branch in me that does not bear fruit, and everyone that does he prunes so that it bears more fruit. You are already pruned because of the word that I spoke to you. Remain in me, as I remain in you. Just as a branch cannot bear fruit on its own unless it remains on the vine, so neither can you unless you remain in me. I am the vine, you are the branches. Whoever remains in me and I in him will bear much fruit, because without me you can do nothing."* John 15:1–5, RSV

Each one of us was made for relationship, crafted in the image of the Holy Trinity. Therefore, we need to do our part in communicating with God on a regular basis. This communication will take on a couple of forms:

We reach out to God when we take the time to talk with Him about our day. We share our joys, our sorrows, our concerns, and the situations in which we are grateful for His fatherly care. We can adopt the acronym ACTS as a simple tool in our personal prayer. Spending a few moments *Adoring* God for His greatness, having true *Contrition* for our failings and sins and making amends not to fall into them again, giving God the *Thanksgiving* that is due to Him for the many blessings and graces He bestows on us each day, and finally placing our *Supplications* (or needs) before His throne. When we include these four areas of prayer into our conversation we give great glory to God and restore that relationship that He longs to have with each one of us.

One of the best ways we can regularly listen to God is by prayerfully reading the Sacred Scriptures. St. Ambrose reminds us:

> *"We speak to him when we pray; we listen to him when we read the divine oracles."*

Our life on earth is to be a great adventure directed toward heaven. Being tapped into God's plan is our sure way to know the path to take in any given situation. Ask yourself, is your life the adventure that you dreamed of as a child? Or do you long for the purpose and adventure God created you for? Only by abiding in His presence will you be able to know His will. By spending time with Him, you will bear much fruit. Yes, there will be times of pruning and struggle, but knowing that our loving Father is in control and has our holiness and best interest in mind should bring us much peace. The world is full of traps intended to keep us so busy that we don't take time to spend with God, but we are ultimately in control of our destiny, and we can make the changes needed to live the life that God has planned for us. He is our refreshment, and He alone gives us purpose and peace in the midst of chaos.

It is important to realize that we cannot give our daughters the faith and confidence they will need in order to succeed in this world if we don't first strive to possess it ourselves. The same is true for maintaining an active and vibrant prayer life; we can't ask our daughters to take time each day to pray if we are not willing to hold ourselves to the same—if not higher—standard. It is expected that a mentor should always ask *more* of himself than he does of his students. All we have to do is look at Jesus as our prime example of this concept:

> *And in the morning, a great while before day, he rose and went out to a lonely place, and there he prayed.* Mark 1:35, RSV

> *And after he had taken leave of them, he went up on the mountain to pray.* Mark 6:46, RSV

> *But he withdrew to the wilderness and prayed.* Luke 5:16, RSV

> *In these days he went out to the mountain to pray; and all night he continued in prayer to God."* Luke 6:12, RSV

He often rose early in the morning to pray, to spend time with the Father in intimate conversation. We can do this too. In the medical field it is often said that if people want to obtain optimal health they should eat like a king in the morning, a prince in the afternoon, and a pauper in the evening. This concept can be applied to our spiritual life as well. If we are to maintain optimal spiritual health, we should feast on time with God in the morning, visit with Him in the afternoon, and say goodnight to Him in the evening.

It is as simple as making the effort to rise thirty minutes before the family to spend some quiet moments talking with our Father, His Son, and the Holy Spirit. Starting with a morning offering and giving our day to God is an easy way to begin our conversation. Then take a few moments and pray through the ACTS method presented above. You will be amazed at how quickly your time will fly by. You will be reenergized to live your day with renewed vision and effort given to you by God. Remember Him at noontime with a short prayer, and connect with Him in the evening by getting in the habit of saying an examination of conscience before bed.

> "Therefore, stay awake! For you do not know on which day your Lord will come. Be sure of this: if the master of the house had known the hour of night when the thief was coming, he would have stayed awake and not let his house be broken into. So too, you also must be prepared, for at an hour you do not expect, the Son of Man will come." Matthew 24:42–44

Getting into the simple habit of doing these three things before you go to bed will help you to always be ready to meet our Lord. In three short minutes you could...

- ✤ Look at your day and see what good you did.
- ✤ Look at the day and admit the things you did that were not so good, having sorrow for them.
- ✤ Make a resolution to be better tomorrow.

This is a simple way to spend one more time with God before the day is through.

Girls' Day Out #3
*Find a Quiet Place to
Pray and Be with God*

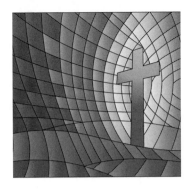

WHERE TO GO

Find a quiet place: a shrine or your church.

Make a visit to a local Catholic church and spend time in front of the Blessed Sacrament, where we as Catholics believe that Jesus is truly present, waiting for us.

WHAT TO BRING

- This book, *Girls' Night Out*
- Journals
- Favorite prayer book or devotional
- *Holy Bible*

What an incredible witness it is to go before our Lord with our daughters. Sharing our faith is one of the deepest connections we can make together. As Catholics, we recognize that Jesus is *truly* present in the Holy Eucharist: Body, Blood, Soul, and Divinity. I know many women who are not Catholic who make regular visits to a Catholic church to sit in the presence of our Lord. It was Jesus' Real Presence in the Eucharist, and feeling His presence in the tabernacle of a Catholic church that brought me back to the fullness of my Catholic faith. Being able to share this union with God with our daughters is a great gift. If you are not Catholic, I invite you to go and make a visit to a Catholic church and sit with our Lord. Talk to Him and experience His presence in your life in a new and dynamic way.

When we do this we are letting our daughters know that we want to be vulnerable before Jesus, and that they too can be vulnerable in His presence. They will be able to see by our example that He desires us to talk to Him and entrust our lives to Him. By spending time in conversation with Christ, He will be able to reveal the Father's plan to each of us. What peace we will know when we live this way!

While in church look up verses that apply to this discussion on prayer.

> *When you call me, when you go to pray to me, I will listen to you. When you look for me, you will find me. Yes, when you seek me with all your heart.* Jeremiah 29:12–13

You may want to make some time for silent prayer for each of you to talk openly to God in the privacy of your heart. You could end the time of prayer by opening your journals and writing as you feel moved. Recording a few thoughts that come to you in prayer is a great way to remember how and what God might be speaking to you. This can serve to establish a habit of keeping a prayer journal for both mother *and* daughter. Close with telling your daughter that growing in relationship with Christ is so beautiful. When people look at her, they will see a life of grace, joy, and peace, and will be attracted to it. This supernatural beauty is highly contagious and more exquisite than mere natural beauty. Thank God for allowing you to grow together.

MINI-BIBLE STUDY IDEAS TO GET STARTED

Great verses to begin with

- ✤ Deuteronomy 4:29
- ✤ Mark 11:24
- ✤ Psalm 145:18–19
- ✤ James 5:16
- ✤ Ephesians 6:18

How did Jesus teach us to pray in parables?

- ✤ Luke 11:5–13
- ✤ Luke 18:1–8
- ✤ Luke 18:9–14

What was Jesus' own prayer life like?

- ✤ Matthew 26:36–45
- ✤ Mark 1:35
- ✤ Mark 6:46–47
- ✤ Luke 5:16
- ✤ Luke 6:12
- ✤ John 17

GIRL TALK

> *Let not yours be the outward adorning with braiding of hair, decoration of gold, and wearing of clothing, but let it be the hidden person of the heart with the imperishable jewel of a gentle and quiet spirit, which in God's sight is very precious.*
> 1 Peter 3:3–4, RSV

After you leave the church, find a place to talk about your shared experience. On the way you might pick up smoothies to sip while you chat together. A walk in the park, a simple hike, or a scenic drive might be perfect settings for drinking smoothies and engaging in some shared reflection.

Talk about the verses you read about Jesus during your prayer time, and think about some personal goals. It is helpful to be very specific: set a time to be with God daily in prayer and Scripture reading. We don't want to be the clock police, so think in terms of your everyday routine. If your daughter spends fifteen minutes each morning getting ready for school, then ask her how much more time she is going to give to developing her inner beauty by growing in communication with God in prayer. You could help her set the goal of spending 15–20 minutes with God before she begins the day. The same principle applies to mom as well. Curtis and I have found it helpful to sit together at the beginning of our day and share quiet time with one another. In the summer, we drink a cup of coffee on our porch and have quiet prayer time together.

Make a deal to hold each other accountable to your prayer time, and perhaps you can even come up with a simple sanction to ensure accountability. It could be as simple as "mom will clean the daughter's room if she fails to make her prayer," and "daughter will clean mom's bathroom or do dishes for the weekend if she fails in her prayer commitment."

Make time once a week, perhaps on a Saturday morning, to come together and discuss your successes and failures at keeping your daily conversation with your Father flowing. This builds a bond and helps you keep one another accountable to this wonderful goal. This open honesty with each other concerning the setting and achieving of your specific goals will further strengthen your bond as mother and daughter striving together to be the best version of yourself that God desires.

JOURNAL TIME

Take all of the ideas and thoughts from your prayers and write them in your journals. After talking together, write down your goals for specific prayer time. Write out and sign a promise to work together toward attaining your goals. Both mom and daughter should sign the promise to try to commit to daily prayer in each journal.

| Here is a sample promise:

I, _____, will try to spend _____minutes a day in quiet prayer and Scripture reading during the next month. I commit to doing this every day of the week. If I miss more than two days in a week, I will _____ for my daughter/ for my mother.

Signed_____

Date_____

PRAYER TIME

Since you had a time of prayer together for this activity, you might want to keep your closing prayer short and sweet. It is easy to say a spontaneous prayer or aspiration, such as "Jesus we love you," before exiting your car. This is a great way to encourage your daughter as she begins this new mature challenge with you. As always, I like to invoke our Lady's motherly care and protection.

> *The Lord is near to all who call upon him, to all who call upon him in truth. He fulfils the desire of all who fear him, he also hears their cry, and saves them.* Psalm 145:18–19, RSV

Read a short essay on St. Rose of Lima and reflect on her relationship with God.

IDEAS FOR BONDING AFTER YOUR DATE

- ❄ Read Super Model: St. Rose of Lima
- ❄ Go on a bike ride if the weather permits.
- ❄ Watch a movie about Blessed Mother Teresa.
- ❄ Read *The Dream Manager*, by Matthew Kelly, and begin a personal Dream Book and a Mother/Daughter Dream Book.
- ❄ If you are Catholic, try to make a date to get to Confession together within the next week. This is a wonderful Sacrament of the Catholic Church in which we believe that the priest sits in the person of Christ, hears our sins, and forgives us in Christ's mercy (Jn. 20:19–23).
- ❄ If your church has perpetual Adoration, sign up for an hour each week that you can attend together.

SUPER MODEL
St. Rose of Lima

Rose was a special little girl from the beginning of her life. She was born on April 30, 1584, in Lima, Peru. She was originally named Isabel but her mother changed it to Rose when she saw her delicacy and beauty as a baby. Her name change became official at her confirmation when she officially took the name Rose. As she grew, Rose's interior beauty surpassed her exceptional exterior beauty. She had a special connection with her brother Ferdinand, but an even deeper connection with Jesus, and she privately vowed to give her life in service to Him at an early age.

When she was six, Rose's family moved to a nearby mountain town called Quivi, where Rose's father had been offered a job running a silver mine. While in Quivi, Rose experienced poverty and faithlessness in the Indian people. After seeing their extreme poverty, she vowed to care for those in need even after her family returned to the city.

Her zeal to care for those in need was accompanied by an industriousness that overflowed into growing and nurturing a family garden, as well as doing delicate needle work. She was able to make good money selling her flowers and wares at the market, and in this way, she helped her family and those in need. Her parents even allowed her the use of a room in their home to transform into an infirmary for sick and homeless people. She found great encouragement from St. Catherine of Sienna, who was not a nun but a Dominican Tertiary (or lay member). St. Catherine's life and writings inspired Rose to walk a similar vocational path. Rose didn't feel called to the convent, but rather, she felt she needed to be out serving and caring for those people in need.

We are told that St. Rose was very prayerful and devout. Many people sought her out for spiritual direction and prayer requests. Although a small woman, she was quite a spiritual giant. Rose became aware of the great deeds that Dominican brother Martin de Porres was achieving in Lima and she wanted to do the same. At age twenty, Rose finally became a Dominican Tertiary like St. Catherine. Rose's parents tried to be supportive of her, but it was difficult for them to understand her vocation of serving those in need. She built a small hermitage on her parent's property and took it upon herself to pray there. She had a very special connection with the child Jesus, and we are told that He often appeared to Rose as she was praying.

When Rose's health became poor, she moved into the home of some dear friends. Rose really lived a life of service and continually grew in interior beauty. She is a supermodel for us today as we try to find ways to grow our own interior beauty.

Lesson 4
Beauty, Purity, and Modesty in Dress

A good wife who can find? She is far more precious than jewels... she makes herself coverings; her clothing is fine linen and purple...Strength and dignity are her clothing, and she laughs at the time to come...Charm is deceitful, and beauty is vain, but a woman who fears the LORD is to be praised.
Proverbs 31:10, 22, 25, 30, RSV

When God created man, He made us in His image and likeness. Therefore, we were made to enjoy all that is good, beautiful, and true. In our very being, we are drawn to be both *with* God and *like* God. When Jesus came and told us to deny ourselves, take up our crosses, and follow Him, He was inviting each one of us to be less like the world and more like Him. Yet we are all broken.

Because of Adam and Eve's fall, we all pay the price and are born broken by original sin and marked by distorted desires—this is called concupiscence. But in the beginning, it was not so; we were made for greatness.

When God created them, Adam and Eve lived in complete peace and happiness dwelling in union with God in the garden. Their minds and intellects had complete governing power over their human desires and passions. It was only when they doubted God and mistrusted His fatherly love and care that they sinned, broke that harmony, and lost that grace. Since the fall, we humans have been born with original sin and an inclination to give into our passions and desires over the better judgment of our intellect. We will forever battle to keep our flesh subordinate to our intellect.

As women we live this in different ways than men do. We must recognize that we are made female and unique, while men are made male and unique. We each share the same dignity and honor as God's children, but we live our divine filiation, or sonship, in distinctly different ways. Women naturally tend towards being more emotional than men, and will struggle with keeping their emotions subordinate to their intellect. We live in a world where we are constantly inundated with what the world (or our culture) says is beautiful, and so vanity is a vice women may be particularly prone to struggle against. Because we desire to fit in and be accepted, we may fall into the trap of wearing clothing that is trendy at the expense of being modest or reflective of God's glory. Modesty is a virtue that results from the cultivation of the virtue of chastity. Modesty is often said to be the "little sister" of chastity, because it is a guard for our purity.

> *"Blessed are the pure in heart, for they shall see God."*
> Matthew 5:8, RSV

If we know that we were made to be with God forever in Heaven, then we need to spend some time thinking about what it means to be pure of heart, and how we are to live this in the present world and share it with our daughters. In the last chapter, we discussed the source of our true beauty. The fact that we are awesome daughters of God is reason enough to relish God's beauty.

> *Do you not know that your body is a temple of the Holy Spirit within you, which you have from God? You are not your own; you were bought with a price. So glorify God in your body.*
> 1 Corinthians 6:19–20, RSV

Our bodies are temples of the Holy Spirit—this alone is reason to know that we are beautiful in who we are—but we need to go deeper. We must strive to recognize that as God's ambassadors for the Faith, we have a royal obligation to live and dress in a way that glorifies God and His kingdom.

We must understand that sharing with our daughters the truth of the beauty and mystery of married love, as God designed it, is not only a great gift, but also a *duty* that we are charged with as parents. We must make use of opportunities to share with our daughters how wonderfully we were made by God and how very different we are as women from men. Hopefully, the time together on this date and following will allow you to talk with your daughter (at her individual level of understanding without injuring her innocence) about the beauty of her femininity in light of a basic understanding of masculinity.

It is a good idea to talk about these things while your daughters are between the age of ten and thirteen, before they've broken out into full, curvy womanhood. Addressing this now alleviates the confusion your daughter could experience if you wait to talk about modesty until after she begins to develop. We never want our daughters to feel as if their God-given feminine shape is bad. They are each a unique, *unrepeatable* part of his masterpiece. If however, this window has passed, take courage, for it is never too late to start investing in your daughter and talking to her about how she is wonderfully made.

Developing your daughter's conscience concerning modesty is a vital piece in helping her develop into a virtuous woman with a strong and positive self-image. Before I go any further, let me clarify that we are not going to be talking about the biology and physiology of married love specifically, but rather about our attraction to one another as male and female persons, and how it relates to modesty in dress.

We want our daughters to realize that how they live now, in the present, will be an integral part of "the gift of self" that our late Pope John Paul II spoke and wrote about so often; the gift that each is to give to their spouse on their wedding night. I want to introduce a psychological theory (Gestalt theory) which I found very helpful when discussing modest dress with my daughter, along with an excellent program which we went through together, taken from the *Secret Keeper Girl Kit*, by Dannah Gresh.

Before delving more deeply into the idea, I'd like to share with you some of the research I found particularly helpful in understanding Gestalt theory. The term "Gestalt" was coined in 1890 by the philosopher Christian von Ehrenfels, and means "experience that requires more than the basic sensory capacities to comprehend."[6] A fundamental principle for a Gestalt psychologist insists that "any whole is greater than the sum of its parts," meaning that the *whole* has properties that cannot be understood simply by analyzing it down to its individual *parts*. A key idea presented by Gestalt psychologists is that our prior knowledge greatly influences our current perception and memory for stimuli. In other words, if we've had a similar experience, or if we are reminded of a past experience, we may unconsciously associate our present experience with such. This automatic "fill in the blank" feature allows the human mind to process information more rapidly, though, as we'll see here, perhaps less accurately at times.

For the sake of discussion, we are going to focus on two of the ways which we cognitively, or mentally, group things or experiences: grouping by *closure* and grouping by *continuity*. Grouping by closure is a result of the tendency we have to want to make our experience as complete as possible—and our desire is to see "wholes" or completions. Humans tend to enclose a space by completing a contour and ignoring the gaps in the figure. For example, closure grouping causes us to see items grouped together if they appear to complete some entity we already know.

In the figures[7] on this page, there is no triangle, sphere, or water, but we will "see" them just the same. Our mind will unconsciously organize items into simple groups according to symmetry, regularity, and smoothness.

The second way to cognitively group is to see *continuity* in images. This might be!

In other words, our mind imposes unity on dissimilar objects and sees continuation where none is directly expressed. In a group of shapes our mind recognizes a complete picture.

While the theory is interesting, my purpose in bringing it into our discussion is that it applies to us today in how we see both things and people. These findings show us that our eyes follow lines to complete pictures in our mind with our imagination. A few good examples: The three curves in a row that look like a worm moving in and out of the ground, "M's" drawn in the sky are understood as birds flying, etc.

Gestalt theory can be especially helpful when explaining to our daughters how men are wired differently than women. Men are more visually stimulated by images than women, and this is not a bad thing! It is by God's design that their brains are wired differently than ours. We do, however, need to recognize and appreciate the differences in perception and response. When men see a girl wearing a short skirt, their eyes will follow the lines right up her legs and finish the picture in their imagination. Women's eyes may do the same thing, but since women are "wired differently," their imaginations don't necessarily complete the picture in the same way a man's will.

For men, the imagination is oftentimes on "autopilot" and they cannot help but see the woman as a whole; therefore, their minds might wander into the territory of impure thoughts when presented with the clothing, or lack thereof, that girls or women wear. Advertisers figured out how to take advantage of the Gestalt theory a long time ago, and our culture is paying deeply for their abuses.

Think about this: If you had a friend ask you to borrow your father's hunting gun because she said she wanted to kill herself, chances are you wouldn't give her the gun at all. Rather, you would assist her in finding help and healing.

This same analogy can be carried over to how we dress. Really!

We should not *want* to dress in a manner that would tempt any man with the means to kill his own soul (which is what cutting oneself off from God's grace by committing a mortal sin does). Instead, we should take preventative measures by dressing with modesty and dignity. For we all know that our souls are eternal and far more valuable than our bodies.[8]

Dr. Alice von Hildebrand is a pioneer in defining true femininity in our age. She has said that since the time when Adam and Eve were forced out of the Garden of Eden, it has become a sign of respectability and distinction to have clothing that veils our bodies. She goes on to say in her book, *The Privilege of Being a Woman*, that anything that is precious, mysterious, and sacred is hidden from view. It is veiled.

In *Dressing with Dignity*, Colleen Hammond includes the following wisdom Muhammad Ali gave to his daughters:

> *Where do you find diamonds? Deep down in the ground, covered and protected. Where do you find pearls? Deep down at the bottom of the ocean, covered up and protected in a beautiful shell. Where do you find gold? Way down in the mine, covered over with layers of rock. You've got to work hard to get to them... Your body is sacred. You're far more precious than diamonds and pearls, and you should be covered too.*[9]

These words of wisdom should ring true in our ears as well. We know that through our Baptism, we are made daughters of God and are holy in His sight. We need to be reminded that our bodies are far more precious than diamonds, gold, and pearls. We also carry Jesus Himself within our bodies when we receive Him in Holy Communion, becoming living tabernacles just as Mary was the first tabernacle. I remember the old days when we would see the tabernacles veiled with silks and lace. Then we moved to a time when the exteriors weren't veiled, but when the priest opened the tabernacle door, we could see the adorning interior fabrics designed to give Him honor. As the liturgical year progressed, the colors of the veils would change, too.

It might be fun on the date for this lesson to look for art that shows the sacred act of veiling the tabernacle. This is a great opportunity to share the vision of honor and dignity that we have as women with our daughters.

Girls' Day/Night Out #4

Book store with café;
jewelry shop or
department store

WHERE TO GO

 ❧ Bookstore with café

It is very common for bookstores to have cafés or coffee houses within the building. Your goal is to find one like this in your area. The plan is to go to the Art history section and browse through a variety of classical art books. Look for Monet, Renoir, Degas, and others. Together with your daughter, explore how women were portrayed in great works of art, and talk about the images and the feelings they evoke. The fun part about the inclusion of a café within the store is that you can buy a hot chocolate or coffee as a treat while you browse and discuss.

WHAT TO BRING

 ❧ This book, *Girls' Night Out*
 ❧ Journals

DIGGING DEEPER

I have compiled a quick overview of women's fashion through the years, gathered from a plethora of sources, intended to facilitate discussion with our daughters as we explore women in art. Take note that traditionally, these fashions were considered appropriate for the honorable "chaste" women. The women who were earning money by living an unchaste life have historically always worn provocative, immodest clothing. Observe how these lines became blurred around the nineteen hundreds.

| Fashion History 101

After they sinned, Adam and Eve made coverings out of leaves, and God clothed them with animal skins when they left the Garden of Eden (cf. Gen. 3:20). From then until Greek and Roman times, the women wore long, flowing tunics that covered their shoulders, and usually their arms, and extended to the ground, along with a veil to cover the head. This was standard dress through the fall of Rome in 476 AD until the time of the crusades. The main difference was that the married women wore their hair up and the single women wore their hair down, though both still wore veils.

In the late fifteen hundreds, fashions became more ornate with ruffled sleeves and high necks, a la "Elizabethan England." One could see class differences, but the long gown and graceful covering still pervaded the fashions of the day. It was around this time that the corset was introduced in order to emphasize the curves of a woman's upper body.

The fashion revolution took place around the time of the French Revolution (1789–1799), when high-waisted dresses with flattened bust lines, long and narrow sleeves, and straight-skirts were introduced.

During this time in the Americas, the waistlines usually fell at the natural waist, with skirts appearing long and graceful. In the mid-eighteen hundreds, skirts became full with hoops and petticoats underneath, as evidenced by Civil War photos.

The nineteen hundreds brought wide shoulders and large sleeves and tiny waists back into vogue, reminiscent of the royal courts of England.

In the early nineteen hundreds, however, things began to change, radically altering six thousand years of clothing trends. It was around the time of the Industrial Revolution, when women began to work outside the home, and the Roaring Twenties exploded into the culture, that we start to see a departure from traditional clothing trends.

Women began to wear short hairstyles, raised skirts, and sleeveless dresses. The 1930s arrived with the onset of movies and the introduction of movie fashions, and from there on out, trends changed quickly. Now cinema had a say in fashion trends. Then came World War II (1939–1945), where women dressed like men in the industrial workplace, but like ladies, in dresses and skirts, when off work. One can see the couture confusion building due to the new roles that women were playing in society.

The first bikini was introduced in France in 1946, but was initially rejected by the U.S. In the 1940s and 1950s, longer, flared skirts and belted waists were reintroduced into fashion, but unfortunately, the bullet bra and push-up bra were also introduced at this time, in order to accentuate the breast line.

In the 1960s, Hollywood introduced a new genre of films including and along the lines of *Beach Party,* and suddenly, portraying bikini-clad movie stars prancing on beaches became very popular. Fashion took a new turn here, with the introduction of very skinny, boy-like fashions for women. Pantyhose were advertised openly, and more and more of the female body began to be exposed in fashion. The blaring colors and jarring images in modern art show how unflattering things had become.

The 1970s brought with them a cultural shift toward women working outside of the home. Here we see feminine fashions begin to take a decidedly masculine approach, leaving some women looking like men. Pants were becoming increasingly popular while feminine clothing was often looked down upon and cast aside as something "outdated" or "behind the times."

In the 1980s, we began to move towards a more casual look. Jeans became the clothing of choice for everyone, both male and female. Big shoulder pads, big accessories, and big hair were all the rage. Finally, in the 1990s, the term "business casual" is coined and touted as appropriate dress in the workplace.

The early part of the new millennium has seen a trend towards the sloppy and "gothic," as well as a style of clothing that leaves little to the imagination. Many young women seem to have no sense of self-worth or dignity as reflected in their dress.

In our present time, the fashion world is dominated by "self-expression," as communicated via tattoos and body piercing. Even many mature women have tattoos and piercings which follow the more youthful fashion trends, and they continue to lean toward the very casual end of the spectrum, rarely wearing dresses anymore. Showing midriff and a lot of skin has become wildly popular. As stated by Mary Sheehan Warren, the author of *It's So You! Fitting Fashion to Your Life*, "Because so much skin is present in current fashion, there is a surge in tattoos to express one's individuality."

GIRL TALK

You might want to begin by talking about how we are wonderfully made, distinctly male and female, by God. Then introduce the Gestalt theory to your daughter. Draw some simple pictures, i.e., M's for birds, the AOL man, incomplete circles and triangles, jagged lines for mountains, and so on. Have her tell you what she sees. Use this exercise to explain how men and women are different in how they finish the pictures in their imaginations. Relate this concept back to our own clothing choices, emphasizing our feminine responsibility to look out for our brothers in Christ.

Tell your daughter that you want to talk about the efficacious power of her beauty by asking what a boy might see when a girl walks by him wearing a tiny little pair of low-rider shorts and a tummy-showing shirt. (He sees past the shirt and shorts and finishes the picture by naturally seeing her body in his mind.)

- ⚜ Can you think of any clothes that you have that might invite someone to finish the picture of you?
- ⚜ What do you think that you can do to avoid wearing clothes that invite people to finish the picture of your body?

- See if you can find any sacred art that shows a tabernacle being veiled with fine lace and silk. Ask the following:
- Aren't we also living tabernacles? How might we veil the Holy Spirit present in our bodies?
- Next, look through some art books to see how women have been portrayed through time. Ask each other:
- What does this say about feminine beauty?
- Is this a beautiful view of femininity?
- How does the portrayal of women in this period differ from today?
- Do you think it would be fun to dress up as the women did years ago?
- Why do you think women make such a big deal about a prom dress or wedding dress?

You might want to talk about God having a spouse already chosen for your daughter. Tell her how he will find her lovely beyond belief and how saving her beauty for him is a true gift and an adventure. This is a great time to introduce the concept of discerning one's vocation. Having a candid talk about married life and religious life will broaden our daughters' horizons for consideration in prayer before God. We will discuss this further in a later chapter.

Feel free to talk about the times that we still should dress up: like when we go to church to meet our God, the King of Kings, or when we go out to a play, to the ballet, or to a symphony concert. Then, talk about times to dress casual, sporty, or professional. We can help our daughters see that we have special clothing for special occasions, and other types of attire for other activities. This knowledge will give her great confidence and freedom as she begins to express herself in her clothing and grows into a young woman.

Take some time to discuss what one might wear for yard work, hikes, baby-sitting jobs, outdoor sports, attending a sporting event, and any other fun ideas you come up with.

JOURNAL TIME

Take time to write about this date in your journals. Share some thoughts about current fashion and about glorifying God in our appearance. Make some resolutions about improvements that each of you can make in your wardrobe choices, and vow to challenge one another in charity when situations arise where good counsel is needed. My daughter has told me more than once that something that I am wearing might not be appropriate for other men besides dad to see… Wow! Out of the mouths of babes! (I went and changed very quickly.)

PRAYER TIME

Before your date is finished, spend some time praying for one another. Share a moment of silence and then offer words of praise to our Heavenly Father for your daughter in her presence. Make a resolution to pray for one another daily.

IDEAS FOR BONDING AFTER YOUR DATE

- ⚜ Read Super Model: St. Maria Goretti.
- ⚜ Go out for a snack together and talk about fashion temptations.
- ⚜ Pray together for courage in shopping.
- ⚜ Go to an art museum and look at women in art.
- ⚜ Go window-shopping at the mall to see what the current trends are before buying.

SUPER MODEL
St. Maria Goretti

Maria Goretti, born in 1890, lived in the small town of Anzio, in northern Italy, with her mother, Assunta, her father, Luigi, and her siblings. After a difficult harvest when the crops had become too thin to live, Luigi decided to move the family south. After moving to Nettuno to become tenant farmers, the Goretti family lived in an old cheese factory and hoped to make a better life for themselves than the one they had led in Anzio. One more child was born there, and while Luigi worked hard in the fields, it was Maria's job to care for the house and baby alongside her mother.

Their family was so poor that none of the children had an education, and were unable to read or write. Assunta, however, worked very hard to teach the children about God and to prepare them for the sacraments. This formation served Maria well, as we are told that she was a hard worker and had a very holy disposition. In 1901, Maria made her first Holy Communion with great joy. Unfortunately, her father Luigi died of malaria that same year. Her mother, sisters, and brother had to work in the fields in his place, while Maria was put in charge of the baby and household chores.

The owner of the farm, Count Mazzoleni, decided that the Goretti family needed help farming his land, so he made them share the large farmhouse with a widower, Giovanni Serenelli, and his nineteen year-old son Alessandro. One day, while Maria was watching her baby sister Theresa and a neighbor's baby, Alessandro, who was captivated by Maria's purity and beauty, returned to the house from the fields. His intention was to take advantage of her, but Maria fought him off saying, "No, no, it is a sin! God does not want it!" Alessandro became so enraged that he stabbed her fourteen times!

When her mother found her in a pool of blood, Maria said "It was Alessandro. He tried to make me do something that was a sin, but he couldn't. I wouldn't let him." Maria was rushed to a nearby hospital, but was near death. Before she died she forgave Alessandro, received Holy Communion, and said, "It is Jesus whom I shall soon see in heaven." When she was canonized on June 24, 1950, Pope Pius XII said that Maria was "the perfect fruit of the kind of Christian home where the family prays. Maria stands for purity, but also for love of the spiritual over the material, docility to parents, harsh daily labor, sacrifice in poverty, and a great love of Jesus in the Eucharist and devotion to his Holy Mother."

She is an excellent supermodel and intercessor for today's Christian youth, who are confronted by the sea of immorality poured out on the world by the modern media.

Lesson 5
Mary as Our Mother and Model of Beauty

This chapter and date are intended to introduce our daughters to the Blessed Virgin Mary as both the Mother of Jesus and as *our* Mother too, that they might cultivate a more intimate relationship with her. We want to instill in our daughters a *confidence* in going to our Blessed Mother for anything and everything.

As women, our Blessed Mother is our finest role model, and inviting our daughters to an intimate relationship with our Lady is a great gift we can give them. An excellent way to cultivate your daughter's relationship with Mary is to give her a love of the Rosary. It might be a good idea to read Pope John Paul II's Apostolic Letter on the Most Holy Rosary, highlighting some of the late Holy Father's most important insights.

> *With the Rosary, the Christian people sits at the school of Mary and is led to contemplate the beauty on the face of Christ and to experience the depths of his love. Through the Rosary the faithful receive abundant grace, as though from the very hands of the Mother of the Redeemer.*
>
> *The Holy Rosary, by age-old tradition, has shown itself particularly effective as a prayer which brings the family together… To return to the recitation of the family Rosary means filling daily life with very different images, images of the mystery of salvation: the image of the Redeemer, the image of his most Blessed Mother.*
> (John Paul II, Rosarium Virginis Mariae, nos. 1, 41)

We have a great gift in the Rosary, but we too often forget how to pray the mysteries. When we pray the Rosary, we pray to God through meditation on events in the life of Christ, through Mary's eyes. St. José Maria Escriva wrote in *The Way*:

> "We go to Jesus—and we 'return' to him—through Mary."[10]

The Rosary is comprised of various elements, intended to dispose us, in an organic fashion, to give glory to God. The prayer is one of contemplation, designed to lead us into communion with Mary. We contemplate the "story of salvation," divided into four cycles called "mysteries." These mysteries express the joy, evangelical life, salvific suffering, and glory of the risen Christ. Our contemplation encourages reflection on the life, death, and resurrection of Christ Jesus and gives us strength to live as his daughters in this world.

We begin with our profession of the Apostles' Creed, and then preface each decade with the Lord's Prayer, which has immense value. Next there is a litany-like succession of ten recitations of the Hail Mary, which is a prayer taken from the angel Gabriel's greeting to the virgin in Luke 1:28 and Elizabeth's greeting in Luke 1:42. Each Hail Mary concludes with the ecclesial supplication beginning: *"Holy Mary..."* This continual series of Hail Mary's is a special characteristic of the Rosary. Each mystery, or decade (meaning ten), is closed with the prayer which begins: "Glory be to the Father, and to the Son, and to the Holy Spirit;" a prayer that glorifies God Who is one and three, as seen in Romans 11:36:

> "For from him and through him and to him are all things. To him be glory for ever. Amen."

Purchase a Rosary pamphlet containing descriptions of each of the mysteries, illustrations, and basic instructions for praying the Rosary to give to your daughter to keep in her journal or Bible for future reference. It would be good to familiarize yourself with the Rosary prayers so that you can model leading the Rosary on your date.

Girls' Day Out #5
Prayer Walk, Church, or Shrine

WHERE TO GO

This date can begin at a coffee shop or restaurant, where you can talk about the Rosary and the importance of having a relationship with Jesus through His Blessed Mother. Once you've had time to talk about Mary and to discuss her role as our Mother, you can decide together where you want to pray the Rosary. If the weather is nice outside, you might choose a park, a walking trail, or a Marian shrine at a nearby church. If the weather is not so nice, you can go to a quiet place at home or to your local parish.

Once you've arrived at your chosen spot, you're ready to begin your prayer time together. Try to pause in imitation of our late Holy Father and state and explain each decade's mystery so that you can really get "into" the mystery as you pray.

WHAT TO BRING

If your daughter does not already own a rosary, then you might want to purchase a special one to present to her as a gift. It could be her favorite color, her birthstone, or something elegant like white pearl. Her rosary should prompt her to think of herself as God's princess, its beads the royal jewels which are entrusted to her care so that she might glorify Him. Ask the Holy Spirit for wisdom to make some spiritual connection when presenting the rosary to her, perhaps emphasizing her purity and beauty as represented in the color or uniqueness of the beads. Have the rosary blessed by a priest before you give it to her, and don't forget to obtain a Rosary Brochure to give her (or make a copy of "Scriptural Rosary," found on page 125 in this book, and slip it into your prayer journal).

GIRL TALK

Before and after you pray the Rosary together, you can talk about how easy it is to talk to our Blessed Mother. Mention that there might be times when your daughter feels angry with you—her earthly mom—and would rather not talk. Point out that she can always talk to our Blessed Mother in heaven. Mary waits to listen to our prayers; the deepest desire of her motherly heart is to bring Jesus to us, and to bring us to Jesus. She longs for our holiness and will help us whenever we ask her.

Let your daughter know that by establishing a relationship with Mary, she is not taking anything away from her relationship with God the Father, with Jesus, or with the Holy Spirit; she is in fact deepening her relationship with the entire Trinity! The Fourth Commandment instructs us to honor our father and mother, and Jesus wants us to honor His mother as our own heavenly Mother. If He didn't, He would not have left her in St. John's charge at the moment of His death:

> When Jesus saw his mother and the disciple there whom he loved, he said to his mother, "Woman, behold, your son!" Then he said to the disciple, "Behold, your mother!" And from that hour the disciple took her into his own home. John 19:26–27

Our Blessed Mother has found great favor with God! The Church teaches of her Assumption, body and soul, into heaven, where she reigns with her Son as Queen of Heaven and Earth for all God's children. We are able to go to her as *our* Queen and Mother and ask her favors just like a child would ask his or her own mom for favors and help here on earth. Mary has the ear of Blessed Trinity in a very unique and special way: God hears her petitions on our behalves because she has proven herself to be a true mother to her children. She who is without sin knows best the heart of God, because she can see Him most clearly. Unfettered by the stain of sin, Mary can approach our Lord directly. When we pray asking Mary's intercession, we do so with the knowledge that she is closer to God than we are, physically *and* spiritually.[11]

You could begin your recitation of the Rosary together by praying to our Blessed Mother as our intercessor, asking her to bring us ever closer to her Son, our Lord Jesus. It might be most appropriate to pray the Joyful Mysteries first, celebrating Mary's willingness to say "yes" to God, and expressing our great joy at Christ's coming because of her willingness to live God's will and not her own.

It's a great idea to commit to saying the Rosary together every week on Saturday, which is Mary's day. Saturday can become a day when the two of you reconnect and spend a few minutes together talking about the previous week and the week to come.

JOURNAL TIME

Take some time to reflect on the twenty mysteries of the Rosary. Write them in your journals and try to imprint them on your heart. It is a great idea to memorize all of the mysteries.

QUESTIONS TO PONDER

- ❀ What are your favorite mysteries and why?
- ❀ What are the qualities or virtues that Mother Mary probably possessed while here on earth?
- ❀ What was she like as a young girl and what might she have been like as a mother to the disciples after Jesus died and rose from the dead?
- ❀ Where did Mary find her strength?

Now ask yourself:

- ❀ How can I be more like Mary in school, with my friends, in the way I dress, at home with my family, and with God the Father?

PRAYER TIME

Take these journal reflections to your final time of prayer. Since our date was spent talking about and praying the Rosary together, you could close with a brief, spontaneous prayer before getting out of the car:

> *"Thank you, Heavenly Father, for the gift of this wonderful time with my daughter. Help us to love You better by imitating Your Son Jesus Christ and His mother, our Mother, Mary. Amen."*

Try to make a commitment to begin praying the Rosary each day. Praying together is wonderful, but praying alone is necessary too. As women, we can gain tremendous grace from our Blessed Mother's protection and guidance in daily life.

IDEAS FOR BONDING AFTER YOUR DATE

- Read Super Model: Mother Mary.
- Make rosaries from kits with friends to give to the poor.
- Plan on saying a decade each day together.
- Make a standing date to pray the Rosary together on Saturdays in honor of our Blessed Mother.
- Look in "Scriptural Rosary," found on page 125 in this book, for the scriptural references to each mystery.
- Read John Paul II's *Rosarium Virginis Mariae*.

SUPER MODEL
Mother Mary

The life and mission of the Blessed Virgin Mary is an amazing story. Mary is a model for every person to follow, but most especially for women. Because of Mary's willingness to say "yes" to God and submit herself to His plan for our salvation, we have our Lord Jesus Christ! There are few words written of Mary in the New Testament, but there is no lack of her presence and importance in Christ's life, public ministry, passion and death, and Resurrection.

Mary's relationship with God was profound and unique from the beginning to the end of her life. God predestined (or chose) her to be the Mother of His Son *before* her conception, preserving her from the stain of original sin. Because she was in a state of "preternatural grace" (as Adam and Eve had been before the Fall), Mary was in union with God the Father at all times.

As a faithful Jewish girl, she was educated about the story of salvation and was open to and anticipating the coming of the long-awaited Messiah. When the angel Gabriel appeared to her, she knew what he was asking and responded with her fiat, "Let it be done unto me." She always trusted God, even when she didn't understand His will. Mary was present at the Incarnation, birth, passion, crucifixion, and Resurrection of Jesus Christ, God Incarnate. She was also there throughout Christ's hidden years in Nazareth, while Jesus was growing and working side by side with Joseph as a carpenter's son.

This ordinary family life and work was made holy and became ennobled by Christ and the Holy Family. The entire human experience was transformed by Jesus living among us. Mary's womb, in fact, became the first tabernacle of flesh holding Christ, and we see that throughout Christ's life, she was constantly redeeming and transforming the world. Mary was the first evangelist, bearing witness of Jesus' Incarnation to her cousin Elizabeth in Luke 1:39–45. Mary is "full of grace," as St. Elizabeth proclaimed. She was willing to sacrifice in order to bring Jesus Christ, fully God and fully man, into the world.

She held Him, nursed Him, groomed Him, and taught Him as only a mother can do. And when the time came for her to offer Him up and trust in God's plan, she did. She opened the door to Christ's public ministry when she asked Him to help at the Wedding in Cana, knowing that their hidden life would never be the same. She gives us the same advice she gave the servants, "Do whatever he tells you" (Jn. 2:5).

At the Cross, when Jesus gives Mary as mother to John, He was giving her to each of us as well. Mary cared for the apostles and she continues to care for each of us as her children. We hear of Mary being present at Pentecost, the birthday of the Church. She understood the outpouring of the Holy Spirit from when she had been overshadowed by His Presence at the Annunciation. Along with the apostles in the upper room, she models for us how the Holy Spirit equips people to live life in complete surrender to God's will.

We too can learn from Mary, and go to her as a child goes to his mother, asking for help, advice, and for greater union with her Son. She will receive our love and requests and take them to God the Father, Jesus the Son, and the Holy Spirit. She is truly our number one supermodel! If we become more like her each day, we will surely grow closer to God and grow into the women that God created each of us to be.

Lesson 6
Fun and Faithful Fashion with Joy

The topic of wearing modest fashions has been a hot one in my work with FOCUS (Fellowship of Catholic University Students) women on college campuses, as well as my work with teenage girls and their mothers. Our girls are constantly inundated with immodest and suggestive fashions by the media and fashion industry. Everything from the television they watch to the magazines they might read all influence them in a potentially negative manner.

The "Be Sexy" message has been peddled by fashion magazines, kids' movies, and television channels like Nickelodeon, the Disney Channel, and Cartoon Network for years. These days it seems that girls elementary school-aged and younger are being targeted for this messaging—and being targeted early.

When you go shopping, pop culture's influence on fashion is evident everywhere. It's easy to see that the "sex sells" motto is driving most advertising, including marketing designed specifically to appeal to little girls. There is an underlying theme that extols "being sexy" as the means to achieve more power or control.

> We can't ignore the clothing battle… or give in to it.

It is becoming increasingly difficult to emphasize to our girls that their beauty begins on the *inside* and is merely crowned by the clothing they wear; that showing every curve and too much skin actually detracts from their true beauty. We are up against a society of incredible influence and means, and we need to be strong in guiding our daughters. As mothers, we can't lose our focus when helping our daughters find cute, fashionable clothing that is modest. It is our duty not only to give our daughters guidelines for choosing age-appropriate apparel, but also to give them our own lived example, thereby driving home the sound principals behind choosing such clothing.

Our culture is pushing skin-baring fashions for young girls, as well as for mature women. We can't ignore the clothing battle… or give in to it. Too many women are buying the immodest clothing that is being peddled to their daughters, but the industry wouldn't be pushing it if people were not buying it. We need to be strong and think outside the box when it comes to dressing with both dignity and style. We shouldn't allow ourselves to be motivated by the fear that our girls won't be popular if they don't conform to these fashions. We need to help them find like-minded friends who are heroically pursuing purity to stand beside them. Our modeling and encouragement will give them courage, and an example to look to when they feel like they are under attack.

We are visually flooded with immodest fashions everywhere; at school, in public, and even at church. It breaks my heart to see my young sons averting their eyes and looking to the floor while we are at church on Sunday mornings because there are so many girls dressed impurely and inappropriately. These girls seem to think that showing their colored bras is more important (and fashionable) than veiling the tabernacles of their bodies.

Our culture pushes a utilitarian image of our bodies; our bodies are primarily for our enjoyment and for experiencing all pleasures at any cost. As a result, some might not think anything is wrong with women jogging in very practical sport bras and spandex shorts, rationalizing that this is "modern" exercise apparel. As daughters of God, we must learn to open our eyes to the reality our culture attempts to distort, recognizing instead that: "No, that is underwear. It is meant to be worn *under* other garments."

Sure, there are different types of clothing for different activities. We have exercise clothes and school clothes, hiking gear, evening apparel and, I would even propose, special church apparel. Our goal as women should be to have variety in our apparel, but always within the realm of modesty.

God tells us that our bodies are not *gymnasiums*, but rather *temples* of the Holy Spirit. At Baptism, the Holy Spirit enters into our soul and takes up residence there. As Catholics, we believe that we receive Jesus' Body in the Sacrament of the Eucharist, and when we do, our own bodies become sacred vessels, or tabernacles, which contain our Lord Jesus. This sacramental understanding of Jesus' Real Presence should affect the clothing choices we make. We want to explain to our daughters and their friends that they are holy beings, daughters of God who are worthy of royal raiment. When we purchase clothing, we want to glorify God *and* the creation He has made. We can't rationalize wearing inappropriate apparel, neither to the Lord's house nor anywhere else, for that matter. It is the responsibility of all women to fight against becoming desensitized by the overabundance of sexually provocative fashion, lest they become "conformed to this world."

> *Do not be conformed to this world but be transformed by the renewal of your mind, that you may prove what is the will of God, what is good and acceptable and perfect.* Romans 12:2, RSV

Christian girls need to strive to please Christ in all things, including the way they dress.

> *Whatever you do, do everything for the glory of God.* 1 Corinthians 10:31

A simple mother-daughter shopping experience can quickly become discouraging. Many trendy stores seem full of clothes designed for strippers and not for our daughters, but take courage! It *is* possible to find modest clothing for you and for your daughter; you will have to look longer and harder, but it is out there. A word of caution: we needn't relegate our daughters to the end of the modesty spectrum, requiring them to dress as cloistered nuns! Our goal is to teach them to dress in a way that always gives glory to God in whatever they wear.

Here are some simple principals that MariAnna and I have learned along the way: Before you go shopping, you need to establish and communicate some simple modesty tests that potential outfits need to pass before they are approved for purchase. As moms know, we are preparing our daughters for womanhood. We will touch more specifically on approaching bodily changes with regards to her fertility in Lesson 9, but for now we'll focus specifically on breast development and other "curves" in relation to modesty in dress. Some of these tests will seem irrelevant to your pre-teen, not-yet-developed daughter, but the idea is to help her develop good habits for choosing modest clothing as she matures. Remind her of the Gestalt theory too.

It is good to get the idea of purity into our heads and hearts now, and to preemptively disqualify articles that may be appropriate to an undeveloped female body, but that we would later rule out as being too skimpy due to her new curves or breast buds (for example: bikinis). It is a great joy to hold one another accountable, and embarking on this adventure is as easy as 1-2-3!

1 Head, Shoulders, Knees, and Toes Modesty Test:

This simple test allows you (both of you) to test clothing for modesty.

- FIRST: Stretch your hands above your head to see if you are showing too much tummy. Tummies are exciting and stimulating, and we want to save showing this part of ourselves to our husband and to him alone once we get married! If too much tummy is showing, then purchase some long t-shirts or tank tops. Many stores now carry longer tanks in a variety of colors, and this is a great way to layer items to cover up while still looking fashionable.

- SECOND: Touch your shoulders with your hands. Can you see your bra or inside your sleeves/arm holes? This too is fascinating to men; if the bra is showing, then it is time to layer or find shirts or blouses that fit more snugly around the arms.

- THIRD: Touch your knees. When you touch your knees, have mom or a friend check to see if you are exposing too much chest skin (or future cleavage). Oftentimes we don't realize how revealing our neckline is to those whom we stoop to interact with. You may need to find a higher neckline, or else continue to layer until you take this test so you don't give others a view of your chest and breasts.

- LAST: Touch your toes. When you do this, make sure that the waist of your pants doesn't show your underwear or too much back/bottom. If you are revealing too much skin, you can try to add a belt, try layering with longer tanks, or find pants that fit you better or have a higher waistline.

2 Skin-Tightness Test

If you can see the outline of your underwear through the pants you have on, try a larger pant size.

If your shirt is so tight that the buttons pull open, or if the shirt springs back like a miniature trampoline when you press the fabric down between your breasts against your sternum, then you know that it is too tight and you need to buy a bigger size.

Remember that we want to cover our bodies in such a way so as not to provoke impure thoughts in others, and to leave something to the imagination for your future spouse.

3 Who Wears Short Shorts: How short is too short?

Remember that the sight of all of your skin is very stimulating. You don't want to show too much. When you are in the dressing room, have mom or a friend help you, or sit in front of the mirror to see if you are showing too much skin. You can pretend to sit, or you can perch on the edge of the bench, and if you see too much thigh or any underwear, then you know it is time to buy longer shorts or skirts. Another great option is to have a little sister tag along. They have no problem telling you if they see your underwear!

These three simple tests can help you find great clothes that are modest and fun!

Girls' Day/Night Out #6

Shopping Together

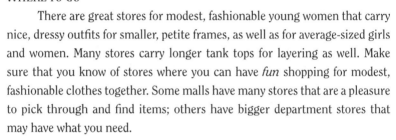

WHERE TO GO

There are great stores for modest, fashionable young women that carry nice, dressy outfits for smaller, petite frames, as well as for average-sized girls and women. Many stores carry longer tank tops for layering as well. Make sure that you know of stores where you can have *fun* shopping for modest, fashionable clothes together. Some malls have many stores that are a pleasure to pick through and find items; others have bigger department stores that may have what you need.

The goal is to go and have fun choosing clothing that is modest and fashionable. It would be a good idea to set a budget before shopping so that your daughter knows how much she is allowed to spend. This is always a delicate issue, because clothing often costs more than we think it would, and is often more than we want to spend.

WHAT TO BRING

- ❧ Money
- ❧ This book, *Girls' Night Out*, or notes on smart shopping!
- ❧ Holy Bible
- ❧ Journals

GIRL TALK

Before you leave (or while in transit) for your shopping destination, you may want to discuss some of the following points together:

- ⚜ Let's put our relationship with God First!
- ⚜ Read Romans 12:2 and talk about what it means to live a transformed life.
- ⚜ Read 1 Timothy 2:9–10 and talk about adorning yourself with godly deeds and what would distract others from God in the way we dress?

Our goal is to get our daughters to understand that we want them to move from a *self*-centered view of life's purpose to a *God* and *other*-centered view and purpose in life. We want them to be able to choose God's law over a fashionable yet immodest style of apparel that would distract or present a temptation to our brothers. All that we do, say, and wear should give glory to God. When your daughter gets up in the morning, she should remember that she doesn't want to wear anything that she would not want Jesus to see her in. As women, we should be proud of the way we look because we are reflecting the love of God as the daughters whom He created each of us to be. Say a prayer each day asking God to help you see yourself as He sees you!

Build Your Daughter's Self-Dignity and Self-Respect!

- ⚜ Read Ephesians 5:8–10 and talk about what it means to be a child of the light.

Clothing is like a label on a brand of jeans; it can give us information about the quality of the product. Our outfits send a clear message of how we value ourselves based on what we look like and on the kind of the attention we can get by wearing the clothes we do. Some girls feel such a need for attention, particularly from guys, that they flaunt their outward appearance and play up their sex appeal at all costs, sending the message that they don't believe that they have inner beauty or anything else worth protecting and saving. It *does* take more self-confidence and inner strength to dress with dignity and grace.

To confront many modern fashions for what they are ("common" and "trashy") and to refuse to stoop to such a low level of dress takes courage.

When a girl dresses with modesty, she is telling the world that she is confident in who she is, and doesn't have the need to flaunt her body to get attention or "fit in." This is what we want for our daughters. We want them to know that they are loved, valued, and worth more than words can describe. Have courage to tell yourself and those close to you that they are worth more than a tasteless outfit says they are!

How We Dress Affects Guys

✤ Read Romans 14:13-21 and discuss how St. Paul calls all Christians to avoid actions that would cause others to stumble and fall into sin.

As mentioned in Lessons 4, 8, and 9, we need to remind our daughters that our apparel has a direct effect on the boys and men in our life. (Feel free to review these points for more information on the differences between boys and girls.) As we discussed, and as many of you already know, boys are more easily visually stimulated than girls. Having seven brothers has been beneficial for MariAnna in this area. When we discuss current skin-baring fashions at home, her brothers don't hesitate to tell her point blank, "If you wear that outfit, you are telling guys that you are 'easy,'" or "You will get a reputation of being sleazy if you leave the house looking like that."

As shocking as it sounds, it is true, and I could not have communicated this to her more clearly or in a more understandable or powerful way. Even though she wanted to argue her point to wear the latest fashion trend, she knew her brothers were speaking honestly and with her best interests at heart. Like my daughter, many girls are innocent in their intentions to wear inappropriate, immodest clothes. They usually don't realize that their clothing (or lack thereof) might cause men to stumble and fall into lustful thoughts. With charity, we need to inform our daughters of the power they have over men. Some are too young to know that their clothing sends a message about who they are on the inside—a message they likely do not want to send. As mothers, we have a responsibility to explain to our daughters why modest clothing is so important.

Have your daughter write this on a pretty piece of note paper to stick on her bathroom mirror as a reminder when she is getting dressed in the morning:

"If I wear this, what am I telling others about myself?"

Impress upon her the reality that if she doesn't want boys looking at her in a sensual way or touching her in an inappropriate manner, then it is her responsibility to cover the parts of her body which quite naturally invite such actions. When we reveal our body to others, it is like giving permission to look and touch us in those places.

JOURNAL TIME

Have your daughter read back through the chapter and write down one Bible verse that really spoke to her heart. Give her time to meditate on it and write a few words of reflection. Then encourage your daughter to write down her favorite parts about this date. Developing an "attitude of gratitude" can be so healthy. Even when we are saying "no" to the cultural trends that don't build up the kingdom, we can affirm the good and celebrate what we *are* able to do with what we have been given.

PRAYER TIME

Take a few minutes to hold hands and pray together before going home. Thank God for the fun shopping adventure together, for your guardian angel's help in finding fun, fashionable clothes, and for His goodness in providing you with the financial means to do a little shopping.

❀ Read Super Model: St. Gianna Beretta Molla.

IDEAS FOR BONDING AFTER YOUR DATE

- ⚜ The Clothing Purge. This can be fun—do mom's closet first! Your daughter will get a kick out of your vulnerability and willingness to take fashion advice from her! Go through clothes together and weed out the non-glorifying outfits.
- ⚜ Continue to go window shopping together and plan modest outfits, just for fun!
- ⚜ Re-work your wardrobe to simplify your closet and maximize your outfits.
- ⚜ Read *It's So You, Fitting Fashion to your Life*, by Mary Sheehan Warren, together. Inside are the Fashion Personality Quiz (also available at marysheehanwarren.com) and a color palette evaluation.

SUPER MODEL
St. Gianna Beretta Molla

Gianna Beretta was born on October 4, 1922, in Magenta, Italy to Maria and Alberto Beretta. As a child, Gianna had frail health, but the privilege of growing up in a large and loving family kept her in good spirits. Maria and Alberto had thirteen children in all, though three were lost to the Spanish Influenza epidemic and another two died in infancy. Alberto was a successful businessman, and while the Beretta family was well taken care of, they chose to live simple lives by following their Franciscan Tertiary training.

Maria and Alberto were extraordinary parents. Each morning they would get up early and attend daily mass together as a couple. As a result, their love and faith overflowed into their family life. Gianna was close with all of her siblings, but shared an especially close bond with her younger sister, Virginia. Her siblings have testified that Gianna lived in the spirit of immense faith, always trusting and accepting God's will. This faithfulness was exemplified by her commitment to doing her best at whatever she attempted. She was not a particularly gifted student, but she studied hard in order to do well in school. She lived believing that holiness consisted in carrying out her responsibilities well.

At the age of fifteen, Gianna experienced tragedy when her sister, Amalia, then twenty-six, passed away. They had been very close and Gianna felt her loss deeply. But her faith seemed to get stronger through this trying time, as she began to meditate daily in prayer and visit our Lord in the Blessed Sacrament. That same year she made a retreat and resolved to dedicate herself completely to her work, her studies, mastering the piano, and joyfully undertaking her household chores. Gianna made a choice to wholeheartedly embrace her single life. When she was in high school, she was very active in the Young Girls of Catholic Action and began discerning her vocation. She was committed to encouraging other young women to be true apostles. In her weekly meetings, she focused on the topics of prayer, grace, and the Eucharist.

Gianna's youthfulness and her faith-filled home life would give her great inner strength for following God's will throughout her life. She understood that even work itself could be a prayer when offered to our Lord in love. Gianna enrolled in medical school, which was unusual for a woman in 1942, particularly during the difficult time of World War II, but Gianna desired to serve the needy through medicine. She wanted to find Jesus in the sick and help people in need, and she endeavored by her work to bring them back to the truth of God's love and mercy. She decided to specialize in pediatrics because she especially loved working with children and their mothers. It was at this time that she thought she might be called to do mission work in Brazil with her brother, Father Alberto, but God had other plans for her. Because she was committed to prayer and was continually asking God to show her His will, she was able to see that He wanted her to marry and be a mother.

At age thirty-two she met Pietro Molla. The two fell in love and married on September 24, 1955. Gianna kept practicing medicine up until her fourth pregnancy. Her love for her husband and children was second only to her love for God. While carrying her fourth child, Gianna was diagnosed with a benign tumor which nonetheless required immediate medical attention. Fearing for the life of her baby, she opted for a procedure which might remove the tumor while still sparing the life of her unborn child.

Her pregnancy continued to term and a daughter, Gianna Emanuela, was born on April 21, 1962. But due to complications following delivery, St.

Gianna contracted a serious infection and fell gravely ill. Despite all human efforts, she died a week later on April 28, 1962. Those who were closest to Gianna have said that she was an intelligent, stylish, elegant, and beautiful woman who loved to smile, loved music and travel, and loved the outdoors. St. Gianna lived an ordinary life in an extraordinary manner. She is truly a supermodel for us women to emulate as we grow in holiness.

Lesson 7
Virtuous Friendships

> *There is nothing so precious as a faithful friend, and no scales can measure his excellence.* Sirach 6:15, RSV

Friendships and peer relationships are a huge part of discovering one's independence and growing up. As our daughters enter adolescence and become young women, we will see a greater need in them to have peers around. It is almost uncanny how they gravitate to others in order to feel "normal" or like they "fit in." It is very important that we give them some guidelines in finding, making, and keeping friends of value, along with instructing them in the art of being a good friend to others. It is all too easy for our daughters to gravitate to the popular kids that may not really be the good kids with good morals and values, but just happen to be in the "in-crowd."

We can help our girls during this important formative period of their lives by encouraging the development of a finely tuned sense of character judgment which will in turn empower them to develop true, life-long friendships. I often think that one good friend is all that my daughter needs; one friend to let her know that she is fun and normal, in all the ways that mom's words alone won't convey. A friend to let her know that she is accepted without condition, and that she is great just as she is.

Particularly during the middle school and high school years, the temptation to follow the crowd will be strong. It is our duty to give our daughters the tools they will need in order to seek out and develop good relationships for the rest of their lives.

My husband gave our children this word picture that I want to share with you in order to illustrate these principles. He asked them if they could tell us the difference between a thermometer and a thermostat. They began to discuss the functions of each tool, stating that both had to do with temperature. After asking a few more questions, we got to the main difference between the tools: a thermometer is the gadget that tells you *what* the temperature is, and a thermostat is the piece of equipment that actually *controls* the temperature.

My husband continued: "Which one seems more important and necessary?" They all agreed that the thermostat is indispensable, especially when it is excessively cold or hot outside. Curtis began to explain that this is also true in the world we live in, pointing out that we each have the opportunity to either be a thermometer or a thermostat in our culture. The kids followed the analogy as he clarified that each of us is given a chance to be like a thermometer in our simple reflection (or mirroring) of the climate of our culture, or to be like a thermostat and actually *set* the temperature of the culture.

When our children are with their friends, they need to be the thermostats! They need to set the moral tone of conversations and actions, so that they may be signs of the culture of life and love that Christ Jesus desires. This is far more difficult than functioning as just another thermometer in the crowd, following along with whatever silly whims another comes up with.

We know that the world is full of challenges for our children. It will serve them well to be prepared and equipped to handle some of these tests *before* they occur. Spend some time developing your daughter's relationship skills—it is an investment that will allow her to experience emotional well-being and peace in relationships as she matures into adult womanhood. This can be especially difficult with relationships between girlfriends.

Because women were made for relationship and are master communicators by God's design, we are especially vulnerable to being hurt through relationships. It seems as though girls experience more difficulties with hurt feelings resulting from other mean-spirited girls, elitist cliques, gossip, jealousy, and hypocritical behavior in peers than boys do. Because of this relational sensitivity, women have to be particularly careful not to fall into sin by their tongues.

> As our culture becomes less and less personal, we become increasingly calloused toward the feelings of others.

We can prepare our girls by equipping them with the proper tools and God's Word to strengthen their hearts for times of trial and

> **We need to acknowledge that the only person whom each of us can control is ourselves.**

decision in adolescence. If we give our daughters Biblical principles to lay for their foundation, then they will be victorious when these inevitable challenges do arise. As they practice taming their tongue and other relational skills, they will become better prepared for living with others in relationships—at home, in college, in marriage, and in the community at large.

We may not realize it, but our daughters are watching and listening to us as they anticipate growing up and making personal decisions. It is our duty to warn our daughters about common issues that come up in adolescent relationships, acknowledging that relationships with girlfriends can be particularly tricky at times, and emphasizing that the key to mastering friendship is first to *BE A GOOD FRIEND.*

We need to acknowledge that the only person whom each of us can control is ourselves. If we continue to strive to become the best friend we can be, then we will survive the rapids in friendships. Allow me to share a few examples of potential problem areas that might come up: As a young girl, I experienced many difficulties in friendship (though by God's grace I had three sisters whom I could always count on as true friends). I was born with physical deformities on my hand and legs, making me a perfect target for teasing and ridicule. I remember countless episodes of great sorrow when mean girls would hurt me physically and emotionally. One time, an older girl threatened to throw mud in my face if I wouldn't show her bully friends my hand; I gave into these humiliations countless times out of fear.

Your daughters may come across "mean girls" as well, and it can happen at school, on the athletic field, or even at church events. These girls usually like to control others and pick on weaker or less confident girls who make smaller, easier targets. They bruise hearts and cause emotional scars by their words and actions. Technology has made harassment more convenient— either by texting, on-line messaging, or through cell phones—and far easier because there is no direct eye contact. Our daughters need to know how to have inner confidence and courage when confronted by a mean girl.

As our culture becomes less and less personal, we become increasingly calloused toward the feelings of others, failing to carefully consider what we think, type, and possibly say. It is not uncommon for parents to check out their children's on-line communication with friends. Take a minute and look at the Facebook page, blog, or personal web page of your child and her friends—you might find out more about your daughter's friends and peer interactions. You can sit next to your daughter at the computer and ask her to share with you her personal page, her friends, and their interactions. She might feel a bond with you rather than nagged by you.

Opening this line of communication between your daughter and yourself is a great asset in discussing character, specifically by examining the quality of her friendships and by helping her to recognize and act upon good relationship decisions.

My mother helped me to be courageous in my own times of difficulty. She strengthened me in God's Word and reminded me many times that God's plan must be great for me if He was willing to allow me to experience these struggles at such a young age. Those pep talks strengthened me and encouraged me to persevere, giving me sensitivity to the sufferings and persecutions of others.

Having virtue is the key to being a good friend, and having one's worth and identity reflect Christ is the best way to grow into the young woman God wants your daughter to be:

> *Do not be led astray: "Bad company corrupts good morals."*
> 1 Corinthians 15:33

I also remember not fitting in with the "in-crowd" of girls in high school. I was excluded for my looks, as well for refusing to participate in the immoral or illegal behaviors that the elite crowd was into. One year, I accidentally got into some trouble with some older kids and was suspended from school for a few days. Unfortunately, I became very popular after that negative incident, but I did not want to be like the elite collection of nasty girls so I stayed out of that clique by choice.

There might be cliques like these at your daughter's school, whose members purposely exclude others and cop a superior attitude in the hallways. There is usually a leader or two with a few followers who follow merely to feel like they themselves fit into a "group." These cliques usually find victims to torment so they can feed feelings of superiority, and sometimes for the thrill of controlling of others. Cliques are different from a close knit group of like-minded friends. It is important to stress to our daughters that having special friends is great, but that the distinctive line between an intimate group of friends and a clique is recognizable in the blatant and intentional exclusion and victimization of others.

Encourage a spirit of charity in your daughter, training her to ask herself in difficult situations, "What would Jesus do?" or "How would Mary act if she were in this situation?" We need to remind our daughters that they are first and foremost daughters of God, and are blessed to be His witness in the world and within their friendships.

> Happy those who do not follow the counsel of the wicked, nor go the way of sinners, nor sit in company with scoffers. Psalm 1:1

Encourage your daughters to look deeply into the characters of their friends. We can all remember times when we shared very personal and private information with a friend or small number of friends, only to find out that our secret was thoughtlessly revealed to others. It is common to have feelings of embarrassment and betrayal after such an experience. If this has not happened to your daughter yet, it will. Once it does, it becomes a great learning tool on how *not* to act within our friendships.

If some of your daughter's friends have habits of gossiping or not speaking the truth, then she can encourage them to be wise and seek God's counsel:

> A perverse man spreads strife, and a whisperer [gossip] separates close friends." Proverbs 16:28, RSV

Or in St. Paul's descriptive warning against evildoers in Romans 1:29–30 (RSV):

> They were filled with all manner of wickedness, evil, covetousness, malice. Full of envy, murder, strife, deceit, malignity, they are gossips, slanderers, haters of God, insolent, haughty, boastful, inventors of evil, disobedient to parents, foolish, faithless, heartless, ruthless.

During our Girl Talk and Journal Time, we will look more closely at the Scriptures to read about an untamed tongue.

A few more obstacles to true friendships: feelings of jealousy, bitterness at that which one doesn't possess which another person does; covetousness, or longing to posses that which another holds, and envy, or begrudging another's good fortune and possibly bringing them harm in order to obtain it for oneself. We all are born with a broken nature; therefore we struggle with comparing ourselves to others according to the standards of the world, even though we know that God wants us to judge ourselves according to His perfection. Our daughters are no different in this arena; they too will struggle with comparing themselves to others, and not only to movie stars, but to other girls they know. As mothers, we need to make sure that we are not modeling jealousy, covetousness, and envy by saying, "I wish my husband was more romantic like that woman's husband," or "I wish my children were better behaved like hers," or "I wish we had a house and more money like they have…"

We might hear our daughters say, "I wish I had so and so's hair, legs, body size, income, personality, etc…" Either way, these are examples of potential jealousy, and when we act upon these thoughts and feelings, we are feeding discontent instead of having an attitude of gratitude for the many blessings, gifts, and talents that God has given each one of us.

We need to remember that we are each unique by God's design; each a one-of-a-kind creation; each distinctive and loved individually by God more than we can possibly comprehend. God our Father has given us all we need to be the best version of ourselves; if we cooperate with His grace and strive to live His commands, then we give Him glory.

As our daughters come to believe in the person whom God made them each to be, the yearning to be another will grow fainter and perhaps eventually disappear altogether. It is our job to trust in God's plan, and to help our daughters to do the same. It is difficult to trust when there are so many ups, downs, and in between, but by trusting we will have greater peace in life. We can better rejoice with others in their good fortune and be content with ourselves and the many blessings, gifts, and talents that God has bestowed on each one of us.

The witness we give our daughters when we live these virtues and share these biblical truths will equip them with the tools they need to pursue interpersonal peace and contentedness. By having goals, dreams, and boundaries for godly behavior, our daughters will be able to take the high road in the friendship department. The bottom line is that nice, godly girls and women reflect the love of Christ in their relationships.

Girls' Day Out #7
Manicure and Pedicure

WHERE TO GO

Make a Nail Spa Oasis in your bathroom at home or go to a nail spa.

My daughter and I found that we actually prefer to have this date at home because we have the freedom to talk openly. When we were at the salon, we couldn't really talk until after we were done with our manicures and pedicures, so I encourage you to consider doing this date at home.

WHAT TO BRING

- ✿ This book, *Girls' Night Out*
- ✿ *Holy Bible*
- ✿ Journals
- ✿ Prepare your bath with nail accessories:
  - · Nail File
  - · Callous Buffer
  - · Nail Clippers
  - · Hand /Foot Towels
  - · Pumice Stone
  - · Hand / Foot Cream
  - · Candles/ Matches
  - · New Nail Polish

GIRL TALK

There is a lot to talk about while you give one another manicures and/ or pedicures, or once you've had them done at a salon. It might be a good idea to reread the issues that most girls struggle with in friendships in order to set the tone for imitation of Christ in our behavior with friends. Feel free to share my stories, or share from your own experiences as a young girl finding her way. Try to highlight the main obstacles that will arise with girlfriends, and talk about possible solutions before they require implementation. My daughter and I have found that talking things out as much as possible helps relationships stay godly and on His track.

It is good to note that many saints came in clusters: St. Francis and St. Clare, St. Therese and her sisters, Perpetua and Felicity, Cosmos and Damian, Timothy and Titus, The Disciples of Jesus. It is as if God wanted us to have companions in serving Him and building His kingdom on earth!

Take some time to look up the following verses together and talk about what they mean and how they apply to our daily living.

> *Where words are many, sin is not wanting; but he who restrains his lips does well.* Proverbs 10:19

> *He who goes about as a talebearer reveals secrets, but he who is trustworthy in spirit keeps a thing hidden.* Proverbs 11:13, RSV

> *"There is one whose rash words are like sword thrusts, but the tongue of the wise brings healing. Truthful lips endure for ever, but a lying tongue is but for a moment. Deceit is in the heart of those who devise evil, but those who plan good have joy. No ill befalls the righteous, but the wicked are filled with trouble. Lying lips are an abomination to the LORD, but those who act faithfully are his delight."* Proverbs 12:18–22, RSV

> *Death and life are in the power of the tongue; those who make it a friend shall eat its fruit.* Proverbs 18:21

"He who goes about gossiping reveals secrets; therefore do not associate with one who speaks foolishly." Proverbs 20:19, RSV

If anyone thinks he is religious and does not bridle his tongue but deceives his heart, his religion is vain. James 1:26

Take courage, for we are told by Jesus in Luke 17:1–6:

"Things that cause sin will inevitably occur, but woe to the person through whom they occur. It would be better for him if a millstone were put around his neck and he be thrown into the sea than for him to cause one of these little ones to sin. Be on your guard! If your brother sins, rebuke him; and if he repents, forgive him. And if he wrongs you seven times in one day and returns to you seven times saying, 'I am sorry,' you should forgive him."

We may need to explain to our daughters that Christ is instructing us to love others by forgiving those who ask for forgiveness, but it is important to let them know that they also need to be wise in choosing friends. If one girlfriend proves herself to be untrustworthy, then your daughter should still be kind to her, but guard her heart and tongue with her so that she does not open herself up for future wounding. Wisdom is a particularly helpful virtue to cultivate when confronting this type of situation.

JOURNAL TIME

▌ Reflect on these Biblical passages and your current friendships.

- ✿ James 3:4–12
- ✿ Romans 1:29–31

▌ Review the passages given in the Girl Talk section. Then evaluate yourself according to God's Word.

- ✿ Has your tongue caused you to get off track with your walking in God's will?
- ✿ How can I be a better friend?
- ✿ How have I been a thermometer with my friends?
- ✿ How can I be a thermostat with my friends?
- ✿ How do I rate with regards to being a gossip? Am I trying to tame my tongue?
- ✿ Is there an older or younger sibling that I could be a better friend to?

PRAYER TIME

Take a few minutes to pray with your daughter for an increase in her self-confidence and ability to have healthy, holy friendships. Let her know that there may be times in the future where she might think you are attacking her or her friends, and you'll want her to remember this date and to trust in your love for her and God's love for her.

IDEAS FOR BONDING AFTER YOUR DATE

- ✤ Read Super Models: Martha and Mary.
- ✤ Arrange an evening to have a friend or friends over to do home manicures and pedicures.
- ✤ Research the virtues in Catechism of the Catholic Church.
- ✤ Saints come in clusters. Find some that were friends and learn about their lives.

SUPER MODELS
Martha and Mary

Martha and Mary were the sisters of Lazarus and friends of Jesus. They were born into an affluent family, and since Martha was probably the oldest of the three, she was therefore placed in charge of the household following the death of their mother. All three siblings were disciples of Jesus, who regularly visited their home in Bethany. Bethany was built on the slope of the Mount of Olives, a suburb less than two miles from Jerusalem and now a part of modern Israel.

Martha is referred to three times in the Gospels: once when Jesus raised Lazarus from the dead, once while complaining that her sister Mary, sitting at Jesus' feet and listening to Him speak, was not helping with the household chores, and once just before Christ's Passion when she and her sister entertained Jesus for dinner. It is thought by some scholars that Mary *Magdalene* is Martha and Lazarus's sister—a woman once lost in sin, then saved and converted by Jesus. She followed Jesus with other devoted men and women and was the first one to whom the resurrected Christ appeared.

Mary had an extraordinary conversion and never swayed or doubted Christ after finding the fullness of life with Him. She spent her life serving Him and telling her story to others in order that they might know Christ and give their lives to Him.

Martha was the consummate hostess, always taking care of her home and guests with great care, and always willing to serve in order to make others feel welcome and comfortable. Martha was challenged to balance all of her chores with spending time with Jesus and others in relationship. She was a strong woman who trusted Christ completely.

Both women understood that it was good to be busy in the service of others and the early church, but they are fine examples of how we also need to remember to keep Christ at the center of everything we think, say, and do. Martha, Mary, and Lazarus did not abandon the apostles or Christ after his Ascension and Pentecost either. They played a significant role in the birth of the Church and the life of the young Christian community. All they had learned from their friendship with Jesus was put into action in their daily lives. They are true supermodels for us to learn from and imitate.

Lesson 8
Boys, Boys, Boys & Girls!

I wanted to spend some time looking at the "Boy Crazy" culture that is surrounding our daughters. Having home-schooled our children through middle school, I'll be the first to admit that some of this is still foreign to me, and I am always shocked when our new ninth grader comes home from high school that first week. It seems that all caution has been thrown to the wind and the girls are all over my sons! I don't know what has happened in the last twenty-five years, but it is as if girls have gone from waiting for boys to call them, to, well, *anything* but waiting. Calling, texting, e-mailing, sitting on their laps, grabbing their hand as they walk along, you name it. We're at the point where all the boys need only to sit back and do nothing.

The girls have usurped the natural leadership roles in the pursuit between the sexes, while the boys are still in shock (and apparently enjoying this new sport). Being boys, they are enjoying the fun, and not having to put their male egos on the line is actually easier for them.

What young women are failing to see is that they are actually depriving these young men of the opportunity to grow into real, live, adult men. By not allowing the young men in their lives ample opportunities to take initiative

> God designed us with particular qualities so that we could better live out His design for humanity.

(read: take risks!), girls who will eventually desire marriage down the road are actually setting their future spouses up for failure in the relationship department. Boys desperately need to put themselves and their hearts on the line for the sake of beauty. When I speak to young girls and their moms, I am always struck by how many of them don't realize that they are actually encouraging the decline of authentic masculinity in our culture.

A girl gets impatient waiting for the guy to make the first move. She doesn't like waiting for a call or a conversation in the hallway at school, so she takes the reins and makes the first move for him. Sounds a bit like Eve in the garden, doesn't it?

We all know that God created two different kinds of human beings: "Male and female he created them" (Gen. 1:27). We sometimes forget that we may need to explain these differences to our daughters because we are living in a culture that insists that men and women are the same.

I want to spend some time explaining some of the basic differences between men and women, so that we as mothers can have conversations with our daughters about these God-given differences between the sexes. Each of us has a particular role to play as unique and precious daughters of God.

I would tend to argue in favor of *nature* versus the more politically correct argument for *nurture*. I don't ascribe to the blurred modern view of the genders, which insists that because we put girls in one environment and boys in another, they turn out the way they do as grown-ups. Research has repeatedly confirmed what any mother could tell you from her own experience: if you put a group of boys and girls into a room full of toys, the girls will gravitate toward the dolls, pretty dress-up clothes, and kitchenware, while the boys will likely gravitate toward the cars, trucks, guns, blocks, etc.

> As a rule, girls are naturally drawn to relationship and beauty, while boys are drawn to danger, adventure, and power.

As a rule, girls are naturally drawn to relationship and beauty, while boys are drawn to danger, adventure, and power. I will even go so far as to say that girls are attracted to what is lovely because they themselves *want* to be lovely. Boys, on the other hand, are attracted to danger, adventure, and power partially because they were *made* to protect that which is lovely from danger.

This is the way God designed us as male and female; these inclinations are built into our nature. Pope John Paul the Great wrote extensively on

> Men and women experience life very differently because our brains, or our central command centers, are fundamentally different.

the beauty of the differences between men and women. He left us some great documents that I encourage you to read if you can: *Love and Responsibility*, *Theology of the Body*, and *On the Dignity and Vocation of Women*, to name a few. I want to emphasize that God created man and woman to complement one another, not simply to imitate one another. He gave us different gifts and strengths, and He wants us each to develop into the women whom He created. Women are generally characterized by beauty, tenderness, gentleness, and that which is lovely, because women are made to reflect to the world these traits found in God. Men, on the other hand, are characterized by power, adventure, and strength (other unique manifestations of God's character) because they were created to protect the beauty and purity of God in the world.

This is not to say that women can't be strong and men can't be sensitive, but simply to point out that God designed us with particular qualities so that we could better live out His design for humanity. It is tempting in adolescence to be preoccupied with thoughts about boys, perhaps even becoming a little boy crazy. Girls seem to giggle and throw themselves at boys in pursuit of attention, and this is not a becoming habit.

In the book, *For Young Women Only: What You Need to Know About How Guys Think*, by Shaunti Feldhahn and Lisa A. Rice, boys were asked about their thoughts on the matter, and they shared some amazing insights that girls can learn from. It turns out that boys actually need to be respected by girls in order to be encouraged to grow into godly men.

My daughter told me that when her dad spoke with her about what boys think of girls who make themselves overly available, "throwing themselves" at the guys they are interested in, she came to understand how unattractive such behavior is.

It is so crucial for us as parents to set a framework for healthy boy-girl relationships, as well as same-sex friendships with girlfriends. Both of these types of relationships will change in adolescence, and a little preparation can go a long way in helping our daughters face the trials and tribulations that will come.

Anyone can see the obvious outward physical differences between men and women, but many don't know (or won't acknowledge) the many internal differences between the sexes. We are different down to our very chromosomal makeup! Men and women experience life very differently because our brains, or our central command centers, are fundamentally different.

After we became engaged, my husband told me that I was the first girl EVER who hadn't tried to kiss him first! The funny thing was, I could think of a couple of times when I had wanted to reach across the car or over the table and give him a little peck on the check—or even on the lips—but for some reason I hadn't. I now know that it was probably my guardian angel telling me not to make that move, because it might have ruined everything!

Curtis has said that he knew he could marry me because he was committed to leading us in our marriage, and he knew that I would be willing to follow his lead. Since then we have read many books and writings on the importance of male headship and leadership by God's design in marriage, and we need to acknowledge that this begins long before marriage, when we are young adults.

So how do we let our daughters know that they are unique and valuable, while not allowing them to become so obsessed with what boys are thinking that they forget to be the best version of themselves that they can be? The answer lies in getting them to focus on who they are, inside and out. If we encourage our daughters to be confident in their individuality and femininity, then they can grow into the women God has designed them to be. We can focus on the positive aspects of self-care and upkeep, helping them to avoid obsessive worrying about boys and what boys are thinking about them.

Let's look at the praise of a worthy woman in Proverbs 31:30:

> *"Charm is deceitful, and beauty is vain, but a woman who fears the LORD is to be praised."*

Our goal is to work on our inner beauty first, without putting too much emphasis on male/female relationships. We need to be fit, spiritually and physically!

FOCUS ON FITNESS

| Becoming Spiritually Fit:

We have already talked about the importance of having a relationship with God the Father, Jesus the Son, and the Holy Spirit; this is the first and fundamental rule of fitness. I encourage you to continue (or to renew) your commitment to spending time each day with the Scriptures and talking with God about life. If this has not become a daily habit, then I challenge you to revisit your journal entry from Girls' Day Out # 4.

There are many devotionals for teen girls that my daughter has enjoyed through the years. It is good to have some devotional to keep you moving in the interior life. As you get more spiritually fit, your confidence will grow and you will be less tempted to be overly concerned with what the boys are thinking and doing and saying....

| Becoming Physically Fit:

The next step is to get physically fit! How are you taking care of that great temple that God has entrusted to you? It can be very difficult to get off our rears and do physical things for fun when the computer and TV seem to call to us whenever we have free time. I suggest that you begin by taking an account of your overall fitness. This ranges from thinking about the food you eat to the activities you pursue to keep you body functioning at top level.

My daughter and I found it fun to do workout videos together or to use the Wii Fit. We enjoyed laughing at the moves mom couldn't do and then the great feeling of adrenaline that comes afterward. Sometimes we treated ourselves to a juice smoothie after we finished—an added motivator! Needless to say, we felt better for having done a workout.

God has cleverly designed our bodies so that endorphins are released when we are actively exercising, bringing feelings of elation and enthusiasm; that's no coincidence! If we are committed to being the women that God made us to be, we need to be committed to taking the best care of our bodies that we can.

Another change mom and daughter can make together is to create a menu plan for family dinners. MariAnna and I both worked on finding fun new recipes that were healthy and looked like they would taste good too. This became a sort of sport for us, and kept our minds focused on growing in grace rather than on the distractions of the world (or the temptation to be boy crazy).

We need to embrace our feminine gifts and grow, allowing ourselves to be stretched rather than giving in to vices. Believe it or not, we now have girlfriends coming over to do workout videos and to bake with us (however counterproductive that may seem). Whatever your passion may be, make that your outlet for healthy living. If you love ballet or dance, then invest in a class. If you love volleyball or basketball, get a net or a hoop and start spending some time outside when the weather permits. Simply put: be active.

Girls' Day Out #8

Work out together or go for a walk in your neighborhood and have smoothies

WHERE TO GO

Go to a local YMCA, community recreation center, your own TV room, or out for a walk in your neighborhood.

WHAT TO BRING

- ❀ Wear your workout clothes and tennis shoes.
- ❀ This book, *Girls' Night Out*
- ❀ Journals

On your way to working out, spend time talking about how important it is to take care of the beautiful bodily temple you have been given by God. Once you arrive at the facility, decide which equipment you would like to work out on. Try to find two treadmills next to one another or two stationary bicycles that are side by side. This will make it easier to talk to one another while you walk or ride.

GIRL TALK

Hopefully by now, you and your daughter have such a rapport with one another that she feels comfortable talking to you about anything. Depending on the school situation for your daughter, there will be differing levels of awareness of the more worldly aspects of our current culture. My home-schooled daughter didn't get a full dose of this phenomenon until she began playing sports at a local middle school. She was a bit shocked at the "boy crazy" attitudes of the girls her age.

> Isn't it cool the way God designed our bodies to celebrate exercise by giving us extra doses of chemicals to make us feel energized and at greater peace within?

We have just talked, talked, and talked it through so that she is comfortable with who she is as a person, regardless of whether or not she acts just like every other girl at school. The fact that some girls your daughter's age may be acting "boy crazy" is something that you can bring up in a casual, low-key way, asking her how she feels about the way some girls act, getting her impressions of her peers. She may be tempted to think that she needs to behave the same way in order to be accepted by her peers, so you may want to put her mind at ease about being different for the sake of the kingdom and encourage her to find like-minded friends to stand with her. She may have friends whom she can cling to for support, and that is great—build her up in this area. If your daughter is struggling in friendships, let her know that you will always be with her as her mother and as a woman.

You may find that during your workout you are too tired or too winded to talk. Don't worry about talking too much; save your deeper conversation for after your workout while you are resting with fruit smoothies. Either way, when you begin talking, just jump right into the conversation and see where it leads. Remember that you might need to guide it, though. Have a game-plan of what main points you want to stress while on this date.

If it will help, write yourself some brief notes. You could start by affirming her in her individuality and stressing God's delight in who she is as a person, assuring her that she doesn't need any boy to approve of her or give her extra attention, because she has the eyes of the Lord on her already. Then, you might review the concepts that we covered in Chapter 3 on the importance of daily prayer and developing an intimate personal relationship with God—Father, Son, and Holy Spirit. Be candid, share your personal successes and failures in this area, and ask her how her commitment to prayer is going. Maybe you need to re-challenge one another to begin again at this great and rewarding task of daily prayer.

After you talk about the demands and practice of spiritual fitness, you might want to talk about the ways that we can get physically fit, always stressing that she is going to gain confidence in who she is as a young woman by challenging herself to be the very best. (Be sure to check with your doctor before beginning any new exercise plan.) Don't forget to talk about the exercise once you've finished your workout. How did it feel to get your heart rate up? Isn't it cool the way God designed our bodies to celebrate exercise by giving us extra doses of chemicals to make us feel energized and at greater peace within? Maybe you could develop an exercise plan and try to hold one another accountable to keeping track of it!

Finally, share some fun ideas of menu planning or keeping fit as discussed in the chapter. Whatever you decide to do, keep the conversation focused on the topics of spiritual and physical fitness and encourage your daughter. This time is supposed to be fun and healthy, yet challenging too. We can all stand a little more exercise and a little less junk food or sweets in our diet, so talk about these areas and about how each of you can not only encourage one another but also plan for personal success by setting and achieving goals.

You might be able to talk about menu planning, shopping for healthy food together, and meal preparation. Invite your daughter to help you in a more active way in this area. Let her know that you need her and that she has a valuable role to play in your family's health. She will

> You may find that during your workout you are too tired or too winded to talk. Don't worry about talking too much.

feel affirmed and probably tremendously enjoy her new involvement in this "grown-up" arena. You might even want to talk about her favorite foods to eat and to prepare. Always remember to share with her from your heart about your likes and dislikes too.

JOURNAL TIME

Encourage your daughter to take a few minutes to reflect on how good she feels after exercising. Write down those thoughts and encourage her to write down some personal goals for living a spiritually and physically fit lifestyle. You could even have her jot down her favorite thoughts about this date.

Examples:

- ⚜ Favorite foods
- ⚜ Favorite exercise
- ⚜ Anticipation for favorite new recipes or responsibilities in the kitchen or around the house.

Encourage her to have fun with growing up, confident in who she is as a young woman!

PRAYER TIME

Before you return home to your daily activities, spend a few minutes in the car or on the couch with your daughter praying for one another, for her peers, and for all the petitions of your hearts. Just taking the time to reconnect with God before entering real life again is a great example of the blossoming relationship that you have with her and with God.

IDEAS FOR BONDING AFTER YOUR DATE

- Read Super Models: St. Francis and St. Clare.
- Go to your local Library and check out some new cookbooks.
- Plan your weekly dinner menu together and make a date to shop for the food.
- Start cooking healthy new recipes with your daughter.
- Start praying for your daughter's vocation and peers together.
- Watch the *Christy* movies together and celebrate friendship and femininity.
- Watch Jane Austen's *Pride and Prejudice* together.
- We enjoyed watching *Julie and Julia* for a fun take on cooking.
- Go out and buy some modest fashionable workout clothes together.

SUPER MODELS
St. Francis and St. Clare

St. Francis of Assisi (1181-1226) was a man completely devoted to God. Francis was a very likable and boisterous boy. He was a leader among his peers, yet not very attentive to real life issues as a child. The son of a wealthy merchant, he lived his boyhood with energy and a desire for pleasure. He was charming and polite and always willing to break out into song in order to entertain others. Though Francis was being groomed by his father to marry into a noble family, he had dreams of becoming an honorable knight and went off to war at a young age.

Francis was captured and thrown into prison in 1202, but was released a year later and returned to his happy life. However, in 1206, at the age of twenty-four, young Francis had a vision that changed his life forever. At the church of San Damiano, Jesus spoke directly to him and told him, "Go Francis, and repair my church, which you see is falling into ruin." After receiving this vision, he radically altered his way of living and devoted his life to living in poverty and working to care for the poor and sick.

Francis's father was very angry with his son's decision to follow God's call and promptly disinherited him. This saddened Francis, but didn't stop him from following God's call to "repair my church." By 1210, Francis had several followers who were emulating his way of life, and he sought and received approval from Pope Innocent III to draw up a rule for his order. He attracted many followers, and in 1212 he was joined by a young lady named Clare.

Clare was born in 1194 into the noble and wealthy Sciffi family. Her father was a count and she grew up in a palace, though that didn't keep her pious mother from passing the Catholic faith on to Clare. We are told that Clare was not only smart but also very beautiful, with long blonde hair. Clare first encountered Francis as she and her mother traveled around Italy to hear him preach. She was drawn to his deep love for the Gospel and his desire to serve the poor by living like Christ. Francis was twelve years older than Clare, but the two became close friends. Both understood the noble call of their vocations, and each was very close to God. When Clare decided to join Francis in his life of poverty, her father became enraged. But Clare held fast to her decision and discerned to start the female branch of the "Brothers Minor," called the "Order of the Poor Ladies."

It was Francis who gave her the simple habit which her order would wear, and Francis who cut her beautiful blonde hair before giving her the veil. Clare was soon joined by her cousin, Pacifica, and other young women. Later on, her sister Agnes, age fifteen, joined Clare and the Poor Ladies. They worked alongside the Brothers Minor doing good works for the poor.

Francis and the brothers vowed to protect the Poor Ladies, and to provide food through their labor or begging; in return, the Poor Ladies did the farming, spinning, and weaving (they made linen for the poor churches), as well as the feeding and caring for the sick and impoverished. We are even told that Clare made a special pair of sandals for Francis that accommodated his stigmata.[12] All members of both communities grew in holiness by serving one another, and most importantly, by serving those in need. Surprisingly, Clare's mother, Ortolana, joined the Poor Ladies once her husband died; mother and daughter doing God's will side by side is a beautiful thing.

These true supermodels show us how great godly friendships and relationships can be. We can always go to these great saints and ask for their prayers when we need assistance in being a better friend.

Lesson 9
Embracing Womanhood and Exploring Vocational Options

God has a unique plan for each of us!

Most people can see the obvious external differences between men and women, but many don't know or won't acknowledge the many internal differences between the sexes. It's more than just appearances: we are different down to our very chromosomes! Men and women experience life very differently because our brains are very different.

Men's and women's brains actually function differently, allowing for each to have particular strengths and weaknesses. Recall that the male mind was formed by God to guard, protect, and provide for that which is beautiful; this intrinsic masculine design allows for greater success in fulfilling the role God designed for men. The female mind was formed for deeper relationship and drawn to beauty, in order to facilitate our unique abilities to mother our children, either spiritually or physically.

It should come as no surprise, then, that men and women deal with life in very different ways. We need to see our differences as our strengths! Dr. Emerson Eggerichs, the author of *Love and Respect*, has a wonderful analogy

> The female mind was formed for deeper relationship and drawn to beauty.

for male/female differences. He proposed that men see with blue glasses and hear with blue hearing aids while women have pink glasses and pink hearing aids. This can make communication very difficult because we see and hear in our own color, and so we need to translate into the color of our spouse. His book was very enlightening and wonderfully helpful.

There is so much more to our differences as male and female than that which meets the eye. Yes, men are physically larger and stronger than women, while we tend to be softer and more delicate. It turns out that our very bodies do reflect, by God's design, our God-given roles as father and mother—we need to acknowledge that we are wonderfully made! In Psalm 139:13–14 we read:

> *You formed my inmost being; you knit me in my mother's womb. I praise you, so wonderfully you made me; wonderful are your works!*

It is fun to note that after God created man and woman we read:

> *God looked at everything he had made, and he found it very good.* Genesis 1:31

God's goodness and His providence for us are revealed in and by His very creation. Our brains show many subtle and profound differences that reflect and support God's design for masculinity and femininity! Both are good—very good—and necessary to living out our divinely designed vocations.

Current scientific research actually supports these intrinsic gender differences, and we now know many specific details of the differences between male and female brains. While still in his mother's womb, a baby boy is bathed in testosterone levels twenty times higher than if he were a baby girl, while her intrauterine bath time submerges her in estrogen—both are stamped with gender awareness by six months in utero; that's three months *before* birth.

One interesting effect of the increased levels of intrauterine testosterone which baby boys are exposed to is that it actually breaks apart certain synapses in the brain, while the fat-soluble estrogen actually allows for *more* synaptic connections in the brain female. Boys in general have 15% less blood flow to their brains, a curious phenomenon which increases the need for more rest for their brain. Adult men come home from work after a long day and want to relax, maybe by playing a computer game or watching TV shows where buildings blow up or cars crash—their brains need a break from all the hard work of the day!

Women, on the other hand, are more likely to sit down to watch a drama featuring a complex storyline, a deep plot, and engaging dialogue between characters. Their brains can handle the depth because they have that extra blood flow! Add to this the fact that male brains have a 25% thinner corpus callosum, which is the strip of fatty tissue that connects the left and right hemispheres of the brain. The larger corpus callosum in the female brain results in a greater ability to process thoughts from the right to the left brain and to discuss the connections yielded!

The male brain also has a smaller hippocampus in its limbic system than has the female brains. This is the area that processes emotional data. So not only is the fluidity of thought in the male mind slower, as compared to the female mind, but the *factory* to process emotional data is actually smaller in comparison. This makes sense when we go back to God's design for our roles.

> Women tend to process emotional data immediately, whereas men need more time to get the same job done.

Women have more fat in their heads, which means more neural pathways to and from the emotive center—the hippocampus. Women tend to process emotional data immediately, whereas men need more time to get the same job done. In *What Could He Be Thinking? How a Man's Mind Really Works*, Dr. Michael Gurian says that on average, men need about seven hours more time to process emotional data. He goes on to suggest that women would do well to give men a "heads-up" prior to discussing emotional data—it will allow them ample time to prepare mentally and physically to do a better job processing it!

I have found it to be a great gift to know that my female mind was designed by God to get the jobs done in life that He has planned for me. Celebrate this reality with your daughter! What does all of this mean when we are discussing vocational options? Knowledge is power; having the power to harness her strengths and gifts will give her greater confidence in her femininity, which in turn will hopefully inspire courage in finding out her mission in life. Let's take a look at two vocational options.

1 God Has a Plan for Married Love!

Now you know! See how amazing the differences between man and woman are, written into the design of our very bodies? Isn't it wonderful to realize, then, that marriage is a tremendous gift from God, as well as a vocation to greater holiness for those who are called? Within marriage, sex and intimacy are beautiful. If you are called to the married life, then God has made you to enjoy your spouse in a unique physical way. Our world has distorted the beauty of God's design by making it seem like physical love is permissible and possible whenever and with whomever we want. This is just not the case with God's plan!

If a woman is called to marriage, then I believe that God has one young man chosen to be her husband. He is preparing him for her, and preparing her for him. It is an incredibly special gift that each gives to the other on the wedding day, and we must strive to protect our virginity for that one special person to whom you will make a gift. Don't let peer pressure persuade you that you were made for common use!

It is critically important to understand the production and the effects of the hormone oxytocin, "a hormone, that acts as a messenger from one organ to another, with specific tasks…oxytocin is released during sexual activity… in addition *to bonding, oxytocin increases trust.*"[13]

It is equally important to understand *why* God made girls this way. He knew that in marriage we would need the extra hormones when we were mothering our children, as well as the resultant extra attachment to our spouse when times get difficult. Our ability to make oxytocin—which is critically involved in attachment—allows us to be better wives, mothers, daughters, sisters, and friends because it equips us to form lasting bonds with the important people in our lives. However, God didn't want us to bond to every boy or person; He knew that when we married, our roles would require us to stay bonded for life.

At any given moment, most women have ten times the amount of oxytocin in their bodies than men do, and there is only one time when men's oxytocin levels are similar to women: during sexual intercourse. God, in His infinite knowledge, knew that men would need to be bonded to their wives! It is so important that we as women understand the power we hold over men and the power they hold over us when we allow ourselves to be physically intimate. Within marriage, this is wonderful and needed, but outside of marriage, these chemical reactions can be devastating to the spiritual, emotional, and physical well-being of both young women and young men.

2 God Has a Plan for His Bride

We have spoken about the differences in the male and female mind in order to give greater understanding to our God-given roles in life. Most girls will grow up and get married, but some will receive a call to an even greater intimacy, and will respond by giving themselves completely to Jesus as his bride. The religious vocation is a great gift, and girls who feel that stirring in their heart when they speak to God in prayer should look into the religious orders that appeal to their charisms.[14]

Many orders have discernment weekends and retreats for girls to experience religious life with the sisters. A great priest once told me that God puts our vocation on our souls at the moment of conception, and that it is a parents' job to help our children hear their call. That has given me much consolation when praying for my children, as I believe that God already knows the purpose for which He created each one of them, and that it is simply my job to help them figure out their life's mission.

It is a good thing to talk with our daughters about this. Encourage them to not assume that they will marry, but to actually get in the habit of talking to God about it, really asking in petition each day for Him to show her *His* plan for her vocation. Another wonderful habit which my mother passed down to me is to develop in our daughters the habit of praying for her future spouse. Whether she marries Christ or weds a man who is merely human, these prayers will reap rich rewards and will also serve to build in her heart a deepening trust in God's fatherly care.

Girls' Night Out #9
Dessert at an Ice Cream Parlor

WHERE TO GO

Make plans to go to an ice cream parlor or restaurant where you can be close to one another and talk privately while still enjoying the excitement of being out on a date together.

WHAT TO BRING

- ❦ This book, *Girls' Night Out*
- ❦ *The Joyful Mysteries of Life*, by Catherine and Bernard Scherrer
- ❦ Journals

GIRL TALK

Let's get ready for the adventure of a lifetime: Womanhood! You might want to share some of the many differences in our brain structure. Giggle, laugh, and praise God for His thoughtfulness and creativity. It might also be fun to chat with your daughter about the many changes that are going to take place in the next year or two in her body. It is great to approach these changes as a gift from God. It is all too easy to grumble about our monthly periods and about our fertility cycle, but we need to live the Gospel of Life by really modeling for our daughters the great *joy* found in our femininity.

Our menstrual cycle is so unique and amazing, as is the fact that God designed us to carry life within our very bodies—what an amazing gift. Now might be the time to talk to your daughter about her upcoming menstrual cycle. Share your own experiences, fears, and stories; she will relish your personal witness and will most likely giggle with you as you share. If you haven't explained how our bodies work, this might be the perfect time to bring out *The Joyful Mysteries of Life*. Tell your daughter that you will begin to read this with her to help her understand God's beautiful design of her physiology and the purpose of married love.

Depending on her maturity and the level of detail behind her questions for you, you can answer accordingly. Ultimately you want to let her know that a key part to her femininity is the ability to carry a child. Her womb prepares each month to receive and cradle a fertilized egg. When that doesn't happen, her body knows to clean itself out by discharging the blood that was to

> Be open and honest with your daughter. Prepare her for these changes and rejoice with her when they occur.

be the first nest for the possible child. Her period is a celebration of the ability to sustain a life. One day she might rejoice in a life moving within her womb. It is easy to explain that there might be a little cramping or pain during the discharging of the blood, but it passes in a few days.

You can also share personal experiences of when you where young and started your period, discussing your use of pads or tampons depending on your age. Be open and honest with your daughter. Prepare her for these changes and rejoice with her when they occur. Let her know that on the day she starts her period, you will celebrate with her. Maybe that can be the day she gets her ears pierced, or you go shopping for a purity ring together. Whatever you decide, make sure she feels loved and accepted and supported by you in all things. When you return home, you might want to show her where you keep the pads, panty liners, and special woman things. Allow her time to explore, feel, and get comfortable with it as well.

Another topic to talk with her about is preparing for the changes in the outward appearance of her body. Her hips are going to widen and she is going to put on some weight, because if she is called to married vocation and motherhood, her body will need extra fat stores to feed the baby while it grows within her and when she nurses him/her as an infant. Her breasts are going to become "breast buds" before they develop fully. She may experience aches as her body goes through these changes, but they are so worth it in growing into a woman. Let her know that she will start to grow hair under her arms and in her pubic area.

My daughter became very self conscious of her leg hair and asked me to teach her to shave. At her first request, I was hesitant and wanted her to wait, but my husband encouraged me to teach her in order to ease her into her body changes. So I put a little planning into a gift basket for her twelfth birthday. I bought a special woman's razor, pretty smelling shaving cream, foot lotions, and band aids just in case. She was so tickled that shortly after receiving the gift, we went to the bathroom to shave our legs together. It was a great time to show her how to shave one row at a time, to be careful in the delicate armpit region, and also how to clean up the sink and bathroom when she was finished! We celebrated our femininity and she felt a little more mature.

This is such an exciting time to celebrate your femininity. There will be many questions, so try to be as open and honest as you can be. Try not to act surprised or shocked, but rather strive to act welcoming in your body language and remarks. Let her know that she can talk to you about anything and everything. Maybe making a date to go shopping for a training bra is in order. If so, make a date to do it soon and then keep your date.

JOURNAL TIME

Take a few minutes to encourage your daughter to write in her journal. She could include things she is thankful for in her girlhood and femininity, as well as write hopes she has for her future. She might want to write a prayer of discernment asking God to show her His will for her life.

PRAYER TIME

As you return home, in the quiet of your car, take your daughter's hands and pray a prayer of thanksgiving for the gift that she is to you, to your family, and to humanity. Pray for her future and for her vocational discernment too. She may want to pray aloud as well. Make sure she is given enough time for this important bonding with you and God.

IDEAS FOR BONDING AFTER YOUR DATE

- Read Super Model: St. Rita.
- Read a book together. Two of our favorites are *The Joyful Mysteries of Life* by Catherine and Bernard Scherrer, about the beauty of married love, and *For Young Women Only*, by Shaunti Feldhahn and Lisa E. Rice. My daughter and I loved reading and talking about these topics together.
- You might want to prepare a little basket with shaving tools, pads, face cleanser, lip gloss, or other fun items that she will enjoy as she enters her teen years and will help her live her femininity with grace.
- Visit Religious orders for retreats.
- Talk to women Religious about vocation.

SUPER MODEL
St. Rita of Cascia

Rita was the only daughter of faithful Christian parents. Her father and mother were simple people who worked the land. They were very poor but knew their faith and taught it to Rita. Rita was a very spiritual child and at the age of twelve she dedicated her virginity to God. Unfortunately, her parents believed that she should marry and arranged for her to wed Paolo Ferdinando, a rather violent young man. The beginning of their marriage was decent—he was intrigued by Rita's goodness and virtue—but he soon reverted to his excessive drinking and bad habits. He took out his frustrations on Rita and she could have been justified in leaving him but she decided to repay his cruelty with prayers, love, and kindness. Ultimately, it was her sincere charity, virtue, and inner beauty that were irresistible to Paolo and led him to a conversion.

Rita loved and respected Paolo and relied on God to help her teach His love and mercy to him. She knew that God would provide all that she needed to survive if she remained faithful to Him and lived her married vocation well. Rita and Paolo had twin sons and began to raise them in the Catholic Faith. Rita wanted them to know, love, and serve God above all else, but tragedy struck their family: Paolo was unexpectedly killed by a rival from his past. The couple's two sons wanted to avenge their father's death and each wandered from his faith. Rita prayed that the boys' souls would be preserved from the mortal sin of killing for revenge. God granted her request by taking their lives through sickness before they could act.

Rita had a very difficult time after her family died, but she found peace through prayer, penance, and works of charity for those in need. She tried to join the Augustinian Convent in Cascia, but was denied entrance twice because she was not a virgin. On her third attempt, the mother superior had a change of heart and allowed Rita to enter. We know that Rita always lived with a joy that her faith gave her. She lived in radical submission to God's will. She married even when did not want to and she obtained holiness for her husband and children by living her vocation well. Her great acts of charity won many souls to Christ and we know that her prayers obtained remarkable cures for those in need. While in the convent, Rita asked our Lord for the gift of sharing in His suffering; she asked for a thorn from His crown of thorns. Christ answered her by imbedding a thorn in her forehead. It must have been very painful yet she embraced this suffering with joy. When she died in 1457 at the age of seventy-six, many people came to pay their respects for this holy woman and many miraculous cures occurred through her intercession. She is known as the "Saint of the Impossible," for she seemed to obtain impossible holiness and impossible miracles for those in need. She is a model for all girls called to the married life or called to the consecrated life.

Lesson 10
Dress-up Date with Mom and Dad

"Blessed are the pure in heart, for they shall see God."
Matthew 5:8, RSV

This last date with your daughter includes her father and signifies his steadfast love and support. By this time I hope you will both be ready to really celebrate who she is as an individual Daughter of God. We want to *especially* encourage our daughters to remain pure. When you go out with your daughter, it is important for you to be comfortable about and rejoice in who she is now, and also who she is growing into as a young woman.

When Curtis and I took our daughter out on a final date in completion of these wonderful talks, we purchased a beautiful set of earrings in her birthstone. It was the first gift of jewelry of any great value that we had purchased for her, and we told her that we knew she would care for them because she was growing into a fine woman. We wanted her to know that though she was worth far more than jewels, she *was* very worthy of wearing these earrings. She already owned a purity ring and we wanted to follow that line of thinking in choosing a meaningful gift fit for a princess.

If she does not yet have a purity ring, this would be a wonderful time to give your daughter such a gift. By hearing your praise and honor, she will be strengthened in her self-identity and more confident in her decision to remain pure. Her future pursuit of purity will be strengthened because she knows that you believe in her.

GIRL TALK WITH MOM AND DAD

Let this time with dad at dinner be a time where your daughter shines! Ask her what her favorite date with you was throughout this program. Share your own favorite date memory when she is finished. Then ask her if she learned anything new about herself that she could share. Have her tell her dad about your mother/daughter dates in general. Try not to interrupt her, and allow her to express herself freely. Even if she didn't like some things or was critical of some of the information you shared with her, allow her the freedom to reflect from her heart. You may want to laugh with her and gently re-explain things if she is confused, but do so sparingly: We really want this date to be the icing on the cake. You might ask her to share other things to get her to open up with your husband:

- ✿ The most powerful thing she has learned.
- ✿ Her favorite date activity.
- ✿ Her favorite date topic.
- ✿ Things she didn't like or feel comfortable with.
- ✿ Things she thinks you should do together in the future to maintain a close relationship.

JOURNAL TIME

Take some time to encourage your daughter to write down the fun things she talked about with mom and dad. Also record your good memories and hopes for the future.

IDEAS FOR BONDING AFTER YOUR DATE

Brainstorm about activities that you have found enjoyable during the process of reading through this program and agree to go deeper into some areas:

- ⚘ Cooking
- ⚘ Working out together
- ⚘ Reading good books together and discussing them
- ⚘ Doing each other's nails on a regular basis
- ⚘ Shopping together

Daddy's Little Girl
A special note for dad, before your dinner date, from Curtis

We as fathers need to see the vitally important role we have in loving our daughters just as our wives do. If your wife has asked you to read this short portion of the book, *Girls' Night Out*, it is because she has been investing in her relationship with your daughter through a series of special times and "dates" together. The time your wife and daughter have spent together has now provided you with a wonderful opportunity to invest in your daughter's life. Each of our personal relationships is sort of like a bank account. We make deposits whenever we invest time, attention and love, but we also make withdrawals when we need to discipline, or make unpopular decisions. Just as with your real bank account, the withdrawals are not a big deal, *as long as you have made enough deposits to cover them.*

Fathers should make an effort to spend some special time with their daughters in order to invest in her as a person. Your time together could be as simple as going for a jog or walk together, or more involved like taking her out to lunch, to an ice cream parlor or smoothie bar, or going golfing. The idea is to *invest* in your daughter's emotional bank account. Both mom and dad have been investing all along by making deposits of time into this emotional bank account that our daughters carry within them. When we make deposits throughout her life, we are investing in her as a person and helping her to have the strength, stability, and courage necessary to be the godly young woman she was created to be. Sometimes this may seem expensive, but knowing that her future success depends upon our willingness to invest in her makes it easier on us as parents to make sacrifices for her, and to make loving her a priority. After all, your time and attention is what she really wants; the real value of any gift is found in the love that it communicates.

Your daughter, like your wife, has been created with an amazing capacity to give and to receive love. As men, we may never fully understand this capacity, but we can certainly learn from it and respond to it. In fact, the key to a healthy and happy daughter lies in her knowledge that she is loved and valued for who she is. Living in this modern world is going to be very challenging for your daughter, and she will be much better prepared to encounter these challenges if she is confident in who she is. For each of us, but particularly for women, this confidence flows from our relationships; both with God, and with those who know and love us best. Your role as her father is to build her confidence, both in your love for her and in her own authentic inner loveliness.

Michaelann and I have had great mentors who have suggested that we maximize our investments into our children by taking advantage of certain special times. At their encouragement, one way that we have done this is by planning a special trip at a key moment in their life that functions as a kind of rite of passage. I have been blessed to have discussions with my sons similar to the conversations in this book that Michaelann has developed for moms and daughters. At the end of this sequence of father/son conversations, I have taken each son on a trip, just the two of us, just as they are getting ready to hit adolescence, in order to celebrate their passage of growth and maturity. Then, later in their lives, it is our plan that Michaelann will take each of them on similar trips shortly after they have left home for college. It is our hope that this time with mom will provide a great start to this next phase of our relationship with them once they are grown. We have made a slight adaption in this plan for our daughter; Michaelann will take her on the pre-adolescent trip as she completes these

> **Your daughter, like your wife, has been created with an amazing capacity to give and to receive love.**

discussions and helps our daughter make the passage into being a young woman, and then I will take her on a trip later after she has gone off to college.

The reason that we feel so strongly about investing our time in our children at different ages of development is because we have found that during adolescence, we as parents have to make *many* withdrawals from the relational bank account. When we say "no" to attending a lousy movie, or when we withhold an iPod or cell phone from a child, we are making withdrawals from their emotional account. We have to make unpopular decisions all the time, and if we don't have a great investment in each child's heart, we might become "overdrawn" in our relational account, which

> The ultimate goal of your time with your daughter is to let her know that you think she is extraordinary and that you love her and only want the best for her, because that is what she deserves.

will make parenting very difficult. Our children have to know that we love them unconditionally and always want what is best for them and for their souls, even if that means that we make an unpopular decision. By constantly investing in our children, by spending time with them and showering them with affection, we are making the difficult decisions easier to handle, offering living proof of our love and desire for their success and greatness.

As men, sometimes we feel like fish out of water when it comes to communicating our affection. Maybe you want to invest in your daughter, but you are not quite sure where to begin. If that is the case, I have written some thoughts for dads to share with their daughters on one such special date.

The ultimate goal of your time with your daughter is to let her know that you think she is extraordinary and that you love her and only want the best for her, because that is what she deserves. Your daughter has been blessed with the same amazing capacity to love as your wife has, and though we men will never fully understand this, we must recognize that in every little girl, God has placed a daddy-shaped hole in her heart; she was made to be loved by you. Even though we can barely comprehend this need, we are called to respond to it. Here are three ways:

1

First, part of being an adolescent will be her own experience of a growing desire for the love of a man. It is imperative that she is confident in *your* love for her, or she will be tempted to turn to other young men in order to find that love she is seeking. This is a critical time in her life; the world will exert enormous pressure upon your daughter to adorn herself with the entrapments of external beauty. Now is the time to encourage her to work on her inner beauty. There is nothing wrong with external beauty—it is a great thing—but if she becomes overly anxious to emphasize only this part of herself, then your daughter will find herself attracting the wrong type of affection. By focusing on inner beauty, you will show her a path that will lead to authentic love and lasting happiness.

Your dates can be as simple as a lunch, a cold drink, or a walk around the neighborhood to talk and connect with one another; just be sure to turn off your phone and give her your full attention. By setting aside time to spend with your daughter, you will develop the habit of sharing life and growing together. Simple gifts can also express the fact that even when you are not with your daughter, you are thinking about her. I have made it a habit that when I bring home some flowers for my wife, I bring home a smaller version for my daughter too. Simple, thoughtful gifts can be a great way to demonstrate your attention and affection.

2

Second, we need to recognize that our daughters will be confronting a formidable challenge: our culture. We need to be sensitive to the fact that we live in an immodest and unchaste world. During adolescence, girls her age will dress and act in immodest and sexually-charged ways, which will provoke a great deal of attention from certain young men. In this culture, a chaste and modest young woman can experience a great sense of loneliness and longing as other girls her age are attracting all of the attention.

Even though the type of attention they are attracting is not wholesome, it will be very appealing; particularly if she is not confident in her inner beauty and the fact that she is greatly loved. It is nearly impossible to overstate the fear of loneliness and real pain of being lonely while others are receiving attention. She will be tempted to dress and behave as they do so that she too will be able to receive the attention she longs for. As dads, we need to let our daughters know that we appreciate the sacrifices they are making. And we need to stress that the man—and the life—she is waiting for are *worth* the sacrifices.

3

Third, we need to explain the differences between internal and external beauty. Tell her that she is a beautiful young lady by giving specifics: "your eyes sparkle like diamonds." Then contrast her exterior beauty with the superior inner beauty of her soul. If we think about it, people have very little control over how physically beautiful they are, but God has given us *immense* control over our inner beauty, the state of our character and soul. Let her know that while you are confident that she could gain the attention of men through inappropriate behavior or dress, if she wanted to, you know that God has something far greater waiting for her. What she is really looking for is a man who will not just be drawn to her physically, but who can truly love her soul *and* appreciate her physical beauty.

Actually, one's physical beauty can become an obstacle—and even a danger—to finding the right guy, because they may be attracted to you for the wrong reasons. It is somewhat like a rich young man trying to find a young woman who truly loves him for who he is and not what he has. He must continually ask himself if the woman is attracted to his money or to his true self. Make sure that you emphasize both, so that as your daughter grows she knows she can work on the external *and* internal self.

> Let her know that while you are confident that she could gain the attention of men through inappropriate behavior or dress, if she wanted to, you know that God has something far greater waiting for her.

The three areas I would suggest that you emphasize for external beauty are modesty, dignity, and grace.

| Modesty

Modesty is dressing and behaving in such a way that people are not drawn chiefly to one's sexuality. Let your daughter know that while everyone knows that she is a beautiful young woman, she will want to dress in such a way that guys don't look at her body and see her as an object; rather, men who are truly worthy will be drawn to look into her eyes and to see her as a person.

> *I adjure you, daughters of Jerusalem. . .Do not arouse, do not stir up love before its own time.* Song of Solomon 2:7

Dignity

Encourage your daughter to have confidence not to overstate her physical attributes through eye catching or revealing clothing, flashy make-up, excessive piercings, and tattoos.

> *"Many are the women of proven worth, but you have excelled them all." Charm is deceptive and beauty fleeting; the woman who fears the LORD is to be praised.* Proverbs 31:29–30

Grace

Remind your daughter that she is an awesome Daughter of God. She should carry herself with ease and grace. Encourage her not to be tempted to exchange her dignity for the affections of an unworthy man. Only a few men on earth are worthy of her love—really only one. Let her know that she can trust God, even in the midst of her loneliness, confident that He will find a way to bring the right man into her life at the right time.

> *Deep waters cannot quench love, nor floods sweep it away. Were one to offer all he owns to purchase love, he would be roundly mocked.* Song of Solomon 8:7

Two areas to stress when speaking of her internal beauty are God's plan for each life and generosity:

God's Plan

Remind your daughter that she was created by God. He had an idea of her in His mind from the beginning of time, and He waited until just the right time to bring her into existence! He made her to be amazing, and He made her for Himself. The love that she wants to receive from a man will never satisfy her unless and until she first accepts the love of God. This can be a perfect time to invite her to give her entire life to Christ; to entrust not only her love life, but every aspect of her being to the Lordship of Jesus Christ. Encourage her to talk to Jesus and allow Him to be her first love.

> *Now this is eternal life, that they should know you, the only true*
> *God, and the one whom you sent, Jesus Christ.* John 17:3

> *For I know well the plans I have in mind for you, says the* Lord,
> *plans for your welfare, not for woe! plans to give you a future full*
> *of hope.* Jeremiah 29:11

Generosity

Encourage your daughter to develop the habit of caring for others. God is love and He desires to teach each of us to be more like Himself. Be generous with others and learn to love as Christ loves.

> *"Give, and it will be given to you; good measure, pressed down,*
> *shaken together, running over, it will be put into your lap.*
> *For the measure you give will be the measure you get back."*
> Luke 6:38

Your daughter's ability to love the man who God created for her is contingent upon her capacity to love others. *Now* is the time to learn how to give generously, expecting nothing in return except being closer to God. This habit of giving of self and learning to respond to others in need can also help ease the pain of loneliness as she waits for the man worthy of her affection.

I encourage you to continue to talk to your daughter throughout her life. She will benefit so much from the gifts of your time and conversation. She may not tell you at first, but the more you invest, the safer she will feel in confiding in you. Enjoy the adventure!

—*Curtis*

Scriptural Rosary
Explore the Mysteries of the Rosary and their scriptural basis.

| The Joyful Mysteries

⚜ THE ANNUNCIATION
The angel Gabriel was sent from God… and when the angel had come to her, he said, "Hail, full of grace, the Lord is with thee Blessed art thou among women." Luke 1:28, RSV

⚜ THE VISITATION
Elizabeth, filled with the holy Spirit, cried out in a loud voice and said, "Most blessed are you among women, and blessed is the fruit of your womb." Luke 1:41–42

⚜ THE BIRTH OF CHRIST
She gave birth to her first-born son. She wrapped him in swaddling clothes and laid him in a manger, because there was no room for them in the inn. Luke 2:7

⚜ THE PRESENTATION IN THE TEMPLE
When the days were completed for their purification according to the law of Moses, they took him up to Jerusalem to present him to the Lord, just as it is written in the law of the Lord, "Every male that opens the womb shall be consecrated to the Lord." Luke 2:22–23

⚜ THE FINDING OF JESUS IN THE TEMPLE
After three days they found him in the temple, sitting in the midst of the teachers, listening to them and asking them questions. Luke 2:46

| The Sorrowful Mysteries

⚜ THE AGONY IN THE GARDEN
"He was in such agony and he prayed so fervently that his sweat became like drops of blood falling on the ground. When he rose from prayer and returned to his disciples, he found them sleeping from grief. Luke 22:44–45

❧ THE SCOURGING AT THE PILLAR
Then Pilate took Jesus and had him scourged. John 19:1

❧ THE CROWNING OF THORNS
They stripped off his clothes and threw a scarlet military cloak
about him. Weaving a crown out of thorns, they placed it on his
head, and a reed in his right hand. Matthew 27:28–29

❧ THE WALK TO CALVARY
And carrying the cross himself he went out to what is called the
Place of the Skull, in Hebrew, Golgotha. John 19:17

❧ CHRIST'S CRUCIFIXION
Jesus cried out in a loud voice, "Father, into your hands I commend
my spirit"; and when he had said this he breathed his last. Luke 23:46

The Luminous Mysteries

❧ CHRIST'S BAPTISM
After Jesus was baptized … the heavens were opened (for him), and
he saw the Spirit of God descending like a dove (and) coming upon
him. And a voice came from the heavens, saying, "This is my beloved
Son, 13 with whom I am well pleased." Matthew 3:16–17

❧ CHRIST'S FIRST MIRACLE AT CANA
His mother said to the servers, "Do whatever he tells you." Now there
were six stone water jars there for Jewish ceremonial washings,
each holding twenty to thirty gallons. Jesus told them, "Fill the jars
with water." So they filled them to the brim. Then he told them,
"Draw some out now and take it to the headwaiter." John 2:5–7

❧ CHRIST'S SERMON ON THE MOUNT
"As you go, make this proclamation: 'The kingdom of heaven is at
hand.' Cure the sick, raise the dead, cleanse lepers, drive out demons.
Without cost you have received; without cost you are to give."
Matthew 10:7–8

❧ CHRIST'S TRANSFIGURATION
While he was praying his face changed in appearance and his
clothing became dazzling white…Then from the cloud came a voice
that said, "This is my chosen Son; listen to him." Luke 9:29, 35

❧ THE INSTITUTION OF THE EUCHARIST
Then he took the bread, said the blessing, broke it, and gave it to them, saying, "This is my body, which will be given for you ..." And likewise the cup after they had eaten, saying, "This cup is the new covenant in my blood, which will be shed for you." Luke 22:19-20

The Glorious Mysteries

❧ CHRIST'S RESURRECTION
He said to them, "Do not be amazed! You seek Jesus of Nazareth, the crucified. He has been raised; he is not here. Behold the place where they laid him." Mark 16:6

❧ CHRIST'S ASCENSION INTO HEAVEN
So then the Lord Jesus, after he spoke to them, was taken up into heaven and took his seat at the right hand of God. Mark 16:19

❧ THE DECENT OF THE HOLY SPIRIT
All were filled with the Holy Spirit and began to speak in different tongues, as the Spirit enabled them to proclaim. Acts 2:4

❧ MARY'S ASSUMPTION INTO HEAVEN
"You are the glory of Jerusalem, the surpassing joy of Israel; You are the splendid boast of our people...God is pleased with what you have wrought. May you be blessed by the Lord Almighty forever and ever!" Judith 15:9-10

❧ THE CORONATION OF MARY AS QUEEN OF HEAVEN AND EARTH
A great sign appeared in the sky, a woman clothed with the sun, with the moon under her feet, and on her head a crown of twelve stars. Revelation 12:1.

On the Communion of Saints

By keeping a statue or a picture of Mary (or other saints) in our homes, we are honoring and remembering our "big brothers" or "big sisters" in our Faith. It is that same human desire for relationship that causes us to hang pictures of our family members—grandparents, cousins, etc.—around our house. We want to be united in prayer and in memory with those whom we love, whether they live here on earth or in heaven!

The unique role which the saints play in the spiritual life allows us to ask these older brothers and sisters in the Faith for "favors" from God. They make up the communion of saints now living with God in heaven, and it is our hope to join their ranks one day too. Their exemplary, holy lives on earth merited for them the rewards of heaven, and the Church has given those of us who comprise the pilgrim church on earth a tremendous resource in their intercession.

This is why we pray for their help; we do not worship them as if they were themselves like God, but we acknowledge that by merit of their exceptional lives on earth, theirs is a special relationship with the Creator.

Endnotes

1   Becky Freedman, *Mom's Everything Book for Daughters* (Grand Rapids, MI: Zondervan, 2002), 22.

2   Freedman, *Mom's Everything Book for Daughters,* 30.

3   Dannah Gresh, *Secret Keeper Girl, The Power of True Beauty and Modesty* (Chicago: Moody Publishers, 2003), 14.

4   Philippians 4:13.

5   Laurie Mintz, lead author of the study and an associate professor of educational and counseling psychology at University of Missouri-Columbia; ABCnews.com, 30 October, 2002.

6   *Seeing the World,* http://iit.ches.ua.edu/systems/gestalt.html (Gestalt, 1993).

7   Public domain, donated by Lehar S. (2003) The World In Your Head, Lawrence Erlbaum, Mahwah, NJ. p. 52, Fig. 3.3

8   Colleen Hammond, *Dressing with Dignity* (Rockford, IL: Tan Books and Publishers, Inc., 2005), 28.

9   Hammond, *Dressing with Dignity,* 29.

10 Chapter 21, "Our Lady," no. 495, available online at http://www.escrivaworks.org/book/the_way.htm

11 Miriam Grossman, *Unprotected,* (New York: Sentinel, 2007), 6-7. See also "On the Communion of Saints," p. 126 in this book.

12 Stigmata: a visible or invisible manifestation of the wounds of Christ.

13 Grossman, *Unprotected,* 6–7, emphasis mine.

14 Charism: a particular spirituality to which a person is inclined, i.e., Franciscans have a charism for poverty.

Bibliography

BOOKS

Armstrong, Regis J., OFM Cap. and Ignatius C. Brady, OFM., trans. *Francis and Clare: The Complete Works*. New York: Paulist Press, 1982.

Courtney, Vicki. *Your Girl, Raising a Godly Daughter in an Ungodly World*. Nashville, TN: Broadman & Holman Publishers, 2004.

Dittami, Mario L., O. Carm. *Family Lives of the Saints, Volumes 1, 2, 3*. Darien, IL: Carmelite Missions, 1978, 1981, 1985.

English Translation of the Catechism of the Catholic Church. Libreria Editrice Vaticana,1995.

Feldhahn, Shaunti and Lisa E. Rice. *For Young Women Only*. Atlanta: Multnomah Books (in Association with Veritas Enterprises, Inc.), 2006.

Freeman, Becky. *Mom's Everything Book for Daughters*. Grand Rapids, MI: Zonervan, 2002.

Giorgi, Rosa. *Saints: A Year in Faith and Art*. New York: Abrams, 2005.

Gonzalez-Balado, Jose Luis and Janet N. Playfoot, eds. *My Life for the Poor: Mother Teresa of Calcutta*. New York: Ballantine Books, 1985.

Gonzalez-Balado, Jose Luis. *Stories of Mother Teresa*. Translated by Olimpia Diaz. Ligouri, MO: Ligouri Publications, 1983.

Gresh, Dannah. *Secret Keeper Girl, The Power of True Beauty and Modesty*. Chicago: Moody Publishers, 2003.

Grossman, Miriam, M.D. *Unprotected, A Campus Psychiatrist Reveals How Political Correctness in Her Profession Endangers Every Student*. New York: The Penguin Group, 2007.

Gurian, Michael. *What Could He Be Thinking? How a Man's Mind Really Works*. New York: St. Martin's Griffin, 2003.

Hoever, Hugo, SO Cist., PhD. *Lives of the Saints for Everyday of the Year*. New York: Catholic Book Publishing Co., 1977.

Hunter, Emily. *Christian Charm Course*. Eugene, OR: Harvest House Publisher, 1984.Kelly, Matthew. *The Dream Manager*. New York: Hyperion Press, 2007.

Kelly, Matthew. *The Rhythm of Life*. New York: Simon and Schuster, 2005.

Lucado, Max and Chris Shea. *God Thinks You're Wonderful.* Nashville: Thomas Nelson, Inc. 2003.

Martin, Celine. *The Father of the Little Flower, Louis Martin.* Rockford, IL: Tan Books and Publishing, Inc., 1957.

Mother Agnes of Jesus, and Michael Day. *The Story of a Soul: The Autobiography of St. Therese of Lisieux.* Trabuco Canyon, CA: Source Books, 1973.

O'Connor, Patricia. *The Inner Life of Therese of Lisieux.* Huntington, IN: Our Sunday Visitor, 1997.

Paul II, Pope John. *Man and Woman He Created Them: A Theology of the Body.* San Francisco: Ignatius Press, 2007.

Pelucchi, Guilianna. *Blessed Gianna Beretta Molla: A Woman's Life.* Boston, MA: Pauline Books and Media, 2002.

Scherrer, Catherine and Bernard. *The Joyful Mysteries of Life.* San Francisco: Family Publications, Ignatius Press, 1996.

Sheehan Warren, Mary. *It's So You, Fitting Fashion to Your Life.* Dallas: Spence Publishing Co., 2007.

Smalley, Gary and Greg Smalley, Psy. D. *The DNA of Parent-Teen Relationships: Discover the Key to Your Teen's Heart.* Wheaton, IL: Tyndale House Publishers, Inc., 2005.

Sri, Edward. *Men, Women and the Mystery of Love.* Cincinnati: Servant Books, 2007.

Therese of Lisieux. *The Story of a Soul.* Trabuco Canyon, CA: Source Books, 1997.

Thomas, Gary. *Sacred Influence, What a Man Needs From His Wife to Be the Husband She Wants.* Grand Rapids, MI: Zondervan, 2006.

Translations taken from The Holy Bible, Revised Standard Version. San Francisco: Ignatius Press, 1994.

Wellman, Sam. *Mother Teresa, Missionary of Charity.* Uhrichsville, OH: Barbour Publishing, Inc., 1997.

Wojtyla, Karol. *Love and Responsibility.* San Francisco, Ignatius Press, 1993.

INTERNET SOURCES

Arbonne International: arbonne.com

Mary Kay: marykay.com

Mintz, Laurie, et al., University of Missouri-Columbia; ABCnews.com, 30 October 2002 (http://www.abcnews.go.com/sections/living/Healthology/HSsupermodel_depressionson021029.html).

National Association of Anorexia Nervosa and Associated Disorders, anad.org